UNDERSTANDING YOUR DOG

JOHN ROGERSON

POPULAR DOGS
London Sydney Auckland Johannesburg

By the same author

YOUR DOG: ITS DEVELOPMENT, BEHAVIOUR
AND TRAINING

Popular Dogs Publishing Co. Ltd

An imprint of the Random Century Group
20 Vauxhall Bridge Road, London SW1V 2SA

Random Century Australia (Pty) Ltd
20 Alfred Street, Milsons Point, Sydney, NSW 2061

Random Century New Zealand Ltd
191 Archers Road, PO Box 40–086, Auckland 10

Century Hutchinson South Africa (Pty) Ltd
PO Box 337, Bergvlei 2012, South Africa

First published 1991
Copyright © John Rogerson 1991

The right of John Rogerson to be identified
as the author of this work has been asserted
by him in accordance with the Copyright,
Designs and Patents Act, 1988

Photoset in Baskerville by Speedset Ltd, Ellesmere Port

Printed and bound in Great Britain by
Mackays of Chatham PLC

British Library Cataloguing in Publication Data
Rogerson, John
  Understanding your dog.
  1. Pets: Dogs.   Training
  I. Title
  636.7083

ISBN 0 09 174579 9

Contents

Acknowledgements

The process of writing a book takes a considerable investment of time, not only in respect of preparing a draft manuscript but also in terms of arranging illustrations, photographs etc. I am therefore indebted to Sarah Buckland (Blue Cross) for preparing the excellent illusrations, to Rosie Hyde and Jim Combe (also from the Blue Cross) for the black and white photographs and to Gwen Bailey for arranging the photo sessions and subjects. I should also like to thank Margaret Smith for assisting in the translation of some of my handwritten text into readable English and Terry Ryan for her valued comments on the manuscript.

I am also extremely grateful to my wife Moira and sons Matthew, Alexander and Marc for their patience and tolerance when I spent hours and hours locked in my office away from family life, working at the word processor, in order for this book finally to materialise.

And my thanks must also go to all of the people and dogs that I have been privileged to be involved with over the years who have assisted me in my quest for a greater understanding of the canine mind, in particular to two friends Sue Megginson and Lester Tucker who are sadly no longer with us, but whose contributions to my knowledge of training should not go unnoticed.

1

Why Own a Dog?

The humble dog has lived alongside man for centuries as a working companion. Being a pack animal like ourselves it has been a fairly simple partnership to establish based on the instincts of the two groups of animals, which are remarkably similar.

Man quickly learned to make use of the dog's superior senses such as smell and hearing and also its better physical qualities such as speed and killing ability. In return for the contribution that dogs made to family life, man provided food, shelter and affection, three of the most fundamental aspects of life, to his best friend. By careful selective breeding, certain physical qualities such as size, colour, coat and overall shape were altered along with the exaggeration of useful working traits such as chasing, killing and guarding. This has resulted in the many highly specialised breeds of dog such as Border Collies, Labrador Retrievers, German Shepherds, Fox Terriers, etc. After producing the type of dog necessary to carry out specific tasks, training techniques were developed to channel all of the dog's energies into doing a useful job of work assisting his new pack leader, man.

When we look at some of the specialist dogs of today such as guide dogs for the blind, hearing dogs for the deaf, search and rescue dogs, police dogs, drug detection dogs, etc., it is easy to forget the common wild ancestry that our dogs share with wolves and jackals. Even though we may have changed the shape, the same basic instincts have been retained by the pet dogs of today.

Man, too, has travelled a long way to reach his present position along the path of evolution and the many scientific and technological achievements made by present-day man would leave our ancestors in complete and utter amazement.

Sadly, as time passes the lives of dogs and man are gradually beginning to drift apart as fewer and fewer people are able to devote the time and patience necessary to understand and communicate with them. Every year thousands upon thousands of dogs are abandoned or sentenced to death for no better reason than a complete failure, on man's part, to understand them. In order even to begin to understand the reasons behind all of the problems that we now appear to have with our pet dogs these days, let's have a careful look at the reasons that people decide to own a dog and, as you will see, sometimes it is the reason itself that causes the problem.

The companion dog

Numerically this is the single largest reason for anyone deciding to own a dog. A true companion dog fits into the family environment and adds a new dimension to family life, being able both to give and to receive affection whenever the need arises. Because of its average life expectancy the companion dog is an invaluable aid in teaching children how to care for another living creature and how to accept the responsibility of raising a young animal who is totally dependent on its pack for survival. As time passes the companion dog's last contribution to its family is to teach them how to come to terms with bereavement.

The ideal companion dog is one that quickly accepts that its ultimate position within the family is going to be on the lowest level in the pecking order. A dog that has designs on being the leader of its family pack, unless brought up correctly, will, instead of becoming an ideal companion, become a liability to own. This means that the initial selection of a puppy is critical if problems are to be avoided and so it will pay dividends to be ultra cautious when deciding which of the many breeds is suitable for the environment in which it is to be kept. There are some breeds that are totally unsuitable for first-time owners and if only people would adopt a more sensible approach and accept that the large guarding breeds that look attractive need more experienced handling and training, then a lot of unpleasant first-time associations could be avoided.

If you own a well-behaved companion dog the chances are that you will tend to get more exercise, you will be smiled at and engaged in conversation more when accompanied by your dog and you will meet more people with a common interest. Anyone living alone and being privileged enough to own a well-mannered dog will tell you that there is no other animal that can compare for offering comfort, security, loyalty, affection and understanding. Our companion dog asks for only a small investment on the part of its owners but offers a huge reward in return for a bed to sleep on, a few games to play, a bit of love and affection now and again and food and water.

Traditionally the small to medium breeds have been kept as companions but lately the trend has moved towards much larger and physically stronger dogs and also, due to the belief that working dogs are more intelligent and therefore easier to train, a growing number of owners are buying dogs with a predominantly working pedigree. In the past a true companion dog would have been selected more because of its lack of working ability than for any other reason. In other words, a companion dog was more likely to be a working dog reject, one that lacked the determination and commitment to be successful at the job of work that it had been bred to do. Just imagine a Border Collie that was totally uninterested in chasing and herding a flock of sheep. If it was lucky it would have been passed on, early in life, as a family pet. In addition to that being good news for the dog it would have been good news for the family concerned because they would have got an ideal companion that was not going to chase the farmer's sheep, the postman or next door's children.

It is a sad fact that there are many thousands of working dogs in pet homes that are subjected to the most appalling mental cruelty because they are kept under conditions which do not provide an outlet for their natural instincts and abilities and then the owners chastise them for the ensuing behaviour problems that arise as a result of denying the dog any form of work or play that will satisfy its desire to do what it was bred for.

The guard dog

The classic guard dog is one that tends to be possessive about its pack and its territory. Dominant dogs are undoubtedly the most possessive category of dog and therefore dominant dogs make the best guard dogs. A feature of our modern society is the number of material possessions that we hoard within the territory of our homes and it is not surprising that because these hard-earned possessions require a means of protecting them from theft, more people are buying dogs with the dual purpose of being guards/companions. Because certain breeds have been selectively bred to produce more dominant puppies in each litter, the chances are that if you buy a guarding breed you have a good chance of picking a puppy that will indeed do the job of work for which it was purchased. The bad news is that although it will guard the house and surrounding territory and all of the owner's prized possessions within, it is just as likely to protect them from the owner as it is to protect them from burglars. It would be true to say that more owners are bitten by their guard dogs than are all other categories of people such as postmen, dustmen, milkmen and burglars put together. Couple that with the fact that a true guard dog will not let anyone into its territory and it's not hard to imagine the owner getting fewer and fewer visits from friends and relations as the puppy gets bigger and stronger and begins to use the skill for which it was bred. The types of dog most often chosen as guard dogs are the large, powerful ones that look the part. The dogs are then actively encouraged to display their natural guarding abilities at an extremely early age, the owners being unwilling to wait until the dog's natural guarding instincts start to develop with maturity. What the poor owner ends up with is a dog that becomes over-enthusiastic about guarding its territory and as a result the owner totally loses any measure of control that he might otherwise have had.

If you think about it logically, a good guard dog is only as good as its bark. If you were an opportunist thief attempting to break into a house and you heard a dog barking at the other side of the door by which you were trying to enter, the chances are that you would desist because of the danger of the dog's barking alerting the owners or neighbours. So the dog does not actually have to be aggressive to be a useful deterrent; it needs only to bark. If on the other hand you were determined to break in regardless of the dog's bark, then even if the dog attempted to bite, it would most likely have little effect as you would probably have arrived at the house prepared to deal with the dog. I will not go into how this may be achieved, as this book is intended for dog owners and not housebreakers. Incidentally, if you own a dog and you want it to protect your home, particularly during the night when you are in bed, then it must have access to all of the areas, such as windows and front and back doors, where people are most likely to break in. Dogs that sleep in the bedroom are extremely unlikely to be effective as guards because as young dogs they would probably have barked during the night or early hours of the morning at the milkman etc., and been told to be quiet in no uncertain terms by the sleepless owners.

The traditional guard dog of yesteryear would have been kept near the entrance to a property, usually fastened by a length of chain attached to a kennel. The dog's guarding instinct would then have developed naturally because it was kept in a small territory (determined by the length of chain), had an exclusive sleeping area in that territory into which no one ventured (kennel, shed, etc.), was fed within the territory and had one or two possessions (bone, stick, etc.) nearby. Although people may have walked near the dog's territory, no one except the owner/handler would enter within range of the dog, the main purpose of this visit being to bring food. The dog, therefore, would tolerate the presence of its owner/handler but no one else. Guard dogs were also kept within fenced-off compounds, the main purpose of which was to keep people out and the dogs in. The Guard Dogs Act (1975) was quite rightly responsible for making guard dogs on any premises without a handler in attendance illegal.

It is an unfortunate fact of life that quite often, after a member of the general public experiences a break-in at their home, they immediately go out and buy a dog for guarding purposes with a view to preventing a repetition of the break-in. The result is that they end up with a dog they did not really either want or need and as it grows it becomes more and more out of control with the result that the police are eventually forced to take action against the owner. And just who was usually responsible for advising the owner that they needed the dog in the first place? That's right, the police themselves!

The dog used for leisure activities

Into this category I would place dogs that are trained for Working Trials, Obedience competitions, Agility competitions and breed shows. Having competed in Obedience competitions, Agility competitions and Working Trials myself, there was a time when I used to refer to my dogs as working dogs, but I feel now that the dogs undergoing training in order for their owners to indulge in leisure activities should not really be termed working dogs. With most competition training, the time spent per week in preparing the dog seldom exceeds a couple of hours. The actual time that a dog is required to work can be as short as a few seconds in Agility competitions, a few minutes in breed or Obedience competitions and up to half an hour in Working Trials.

There can be little doubt that putting an element of competition into training activities quite definitely improves training techniques and from that standpoint it is very pleasing to watch the trend in training moving away from the more negative, compulsive methods of the recent past, towards the better system of positive, rewarding training techniques which are geared towards motivating both dog and handler. I can remember the days when Obedience competitors (including myself at the time) would deliberately get the dog to make a mistake just before entering the ring and immediately 'correct' it on the assumption that the dog would then try hard not to make the same mistake whilst working in the competition when being judged. Happily, now handlers are more likely to tease their dogs with a toy before entering the ring. The shift in emphasis from correction to reward training should give other breeds a chance of breaking the monopoly that Border Collie types have on competition Obedience where the very nature of the exercises make them more suitable to this one breed than to any other. As Working Trials exercises and Agility tests tend to be more creative, they tend to be suited to a greater number of breeds. The reason that most people compete with their dogs is to obtain a comparison of their own training against either other competitors or against a standard laid down by the Kennel Club. Competitions are also a wonderful social gathering of dog owners, all with a common interest and desire for improvement. Competitors enjoy not only working their dogs but also the social side of shows; coming home with a first place or a qualification has always been seen as an added bonus after an enjoyable day or weekend in the company of fellow enthusiasts. As with any other form of sport there is always a small minority whose sole purpose of attending shows is to win at all costs, with the dog merely being used as a tool to satisfy the owner's ambitions. Fortunately the vast majority do compete in the true spirit intended by the Kennel Club when they formulated the various tests and standards relating to shows.

Most people who get hooked on competition training are unlike the average dog owner in as much as they usually own two or more dogs, which brings with it a set of rather unique problems (see Chapter 6, Owning More than One Dog).

The personal protection dog

With crimes of violence on the increase, a growing number of potential victims are now realising the possible advantages of owning a dog with the purpose of protecting them. As with our friend the guard dog, the types most in demand for personal protection are the larger, more dominant ones, usually males.

Once an owner buys a puppy with the intention of it growing up to be some sort of a 'minder' they will generally encourage the type of game that promotes biting and growling, namely tug-of-war. If we look at the natural progression of this type of game (see Chapter 7, Dog/Human Aggression Problems) it is not hard to understand why so many people are bitten by the dog that is supposed to be protecting them. There are three ways of obtaining a personal protection dog: you can buy one ready trained, send your own dog away for training or train it yourself. Obtaining a dog ready trained is probably the worst of the three options because, even though you may be asked to pay

a sum of money around the four-figure mark, it is extremely
unlikely that the dog will have undergone much in the way of
training at all. The majority of dogs that end up being sold as
protection dogs are ones that have been given by their original
owners because they proved too difficult to control and were
generally over-protective. There are a great many so-called
trainers who take in what I would describe as problem dogs
without paying a penny for them and then sell them at fantastic
profits to people who know practically nothing about dogs,
describing them as 'protection trained'. What the unsuspecting
buyer often purchases is a nervous, aggressive dog that will not
let anyone near it or its lead; holding on to the lead therefore
affords a measure of protection to the handler. There are, of
course, a few really excellent trainers who train and sell
protection dogs, but for every good one there must be at least
fifty bad ones. Buying a dog that has already learned to use its
teeth, whether by intentional training or otherwise, is not a
particularly good way of entering into a relationship.

The problems of having your own dog protection trained are
slightly reduced because at least you have the advantage of
knowing the dog quite well beforehand. Once again the
problem is to find a reputable trainer among all of the cowboys
who operate under the name of professional trainers. The
majority of protection training consists of holding the dog on a
lead and agitating it with a stick or cane until it is incited to
move forward and bite in order to prevent its front legs being
struck. The dog thus learns to bark and bite in order to protect
itself and, coincidentally, to protect the person who is holding
on to the end of the lead. It goes without saying that the most
suitable subjects for this sort of training are the more dominant
dogs. The main problem with this system of training is that,
because the owner would seldom have the same measure of
control as the trainer instills, the dog often starts to apply the
training indiscriminately and the owner quickly loses control.
The other problem is that as the owner is unlikely to maintain
the training on a regular basis, the dog's response to the
commands diminishes rapidly.

How about training the dog yourself? My advice would be,
do not even think about it! Attempting to train a dog by playing
wrestling games, tug-of-war and encouraging it to bite your

own arm will result in a dog that, instead of protecting you when you are attacked, will do exactly as you have trained it to do – bite *you*. Just think about it; police dogs are trained to bark at and bite criminals, so the handler instills the necessary control and then other officers dress up and act as 'criminals' for the purposes of training. It is the acting 'criminal' who trains the dog to bite and not the handler, whose only function in the early stages is to apply control and encouragement at the correct times. Start off with a dominant dog and play strength games with it, then encourage it to bite your arms and you are likely to end up in hospital and your protection dog on a one-way trip to the vet.

The working dog

Into this category I would place police dogs, guide dogs for the blind, search and rescue dogs, assistance dogs for the disabled, hearing dogs for the deaf, drug detection dogs and all other dogs that work on a regular basis assisting their owners in their job of work, such as farm dogs and gamekeepers' dogs. Because of the tremendous amount of work that goes into training a working dog, the selection process becomes critical as it would be uneconomical to start training a dog only to reject it as being unsuitable at a later stage.

Some of the attributes of a good working dog are endurance, persistence and concentration. A Border Collie working sheep would be pretty useless if, after running two miles, it was exhausted to the point where it was unable to continue working. On a farm in the Peak District of Derbyshire a Border Collie was measured as covering in excess of seventy miles in an average working day.

A dog used for drug detection work needs to be extremely persistent because it will have to check an awful lot of possible locations without finding anything and will be successful only on infrequent occasions. The dog would be useless if it lost all interest after being asked to check only one or two locations.

Can you imagine the concentration necessary to track a criminal from the scene of a crime for miles across varying terrain? The track may be several hours old and the dog is required to follow only the smell on the ground left as a result of the criminal's feet coming into contact with this surface. A dog that lacks the necessary powers of concentration would be very quickly rejected from the police basic training course.

The characteristics of endurance, persistence and concentration necessary in a good working dog are in evidence if we watch a litter of puppies bred from working stock. The best puppies never tire of playing, are very competitive, have a single-minded approach to games and really sparkle when the opportunity arises to expand their knowledge.

The problem is, of course, that if we buy a dog that was bred to be capable of running seventy miles each day and allow it only two half-mile walks on the lead each day, then even if it is socialised correctly, fed well and given the best veterinary attention, we will surely end up with behaviour problems. A puppy that is extremely persistent in getting what it wants and is capable of concentrating on a single objective for extended periods of time, although a desirable quality in a working dog, would be an absolute nightmare in a pet environment.

I have known dogs that have managed the most incredible escape acts that would have left even the great Houdini mystified. Take for instance the Border Collie that carefully chewed its way around a six-foot by four-foot window surround whilst standing on the kitchen sink until the entire window fell out, thereby allowing the dog access to his favourite doggy friend outside. The escape took several hours of effort, persistence and concentration. Unlike me, however, the owner was not impressed!

Most working dogs do not take an active role in their area of work until they are beginning to mature at around eighteen months of age. If they were worked any earlier they would lack the concentration and experience necessary to carry out their duties with any confidence. Due to the specific requirements of police and guide dogs and the difficulty of obtaining suitable dogs for training, both establishments operate their own breeding programmes aimed at producing dogs of a specific type and temperament for their needs. In selecting a working dog, considerations such as health and fitness for purpose have to be taken into account. Obtaining a good, sound, working dog seems to be getting more and more difficult these days, particularly if you are looking for one of the larger breeds.

Status and ego

It is a sad fact that a small percentage of dogs are purchased both as status symbols and to inflate their owner's ego. If you walked through a fairly exclusive private housing estate ten years ago you would have seen residents competing for the best-kept lawn, the best rose bushes, the newest and most expensive car and the best pedigree dog, which due to the way that a certain brand of paint was being advertised, would usually be an Old English Sheepdog. Not being content with just any Old English Sheepdog, our status-seeking young couple had to have the dog that was used in the advertisement named on their dog's pedigree. Points were, of course, scored if the commercial's dog was the grandfather or better still the father of the new acquisition.

At the present time, if you want to see any of the very rare breeds then go along to the same private housing estates. The fewer the number of a particular breed there are in the country, the higher they are prized by our status-seeking individuals ('bet you don't know what breed this is' is a phrase that I hear more and more). Simply reading the way that some rare breeds are now being advertised as 'exotic breeds' indicates the market that these dogs are fulfilling. Recent adverts name dogs such as Japanese Akitas as 'real head turners'; Shar-Peis as 'attention getters'; Anatolian Shepherd dogs as 'very flashy', and Italian Spinone as 'rare and unusual'. What our status-seeking pet dog owners perhaps do not realise is that the 'special edition' puppy that they have just purchased is in fact related to the mongrel down the road and that even though they have parted with a large amount of money to buy this rare or exotic breed, it is first and foremost a dog the same as any other with the same basic requirements as the mongrel down the road.

Owning a dog to inflate your own ego or as a status symbol is one of the worst reasons for owning a dog. Just ask the Rottweiler or Old English Sheepdog rescue organisations who have to pick up the pieces when dogs purchased for the wrong reasons are disposed of by their owners because they have become 'difficult'.

Financial gain

Some people, quite legitimately, make money as a result of owning dogs. People such as professional breeders, after paying out fees for the best stud dogs, importing good breeding stock, vaccinations, feeding, insurance, maintenance, etc., sometimes end up with a small profit for their efforts. A good breeder will invariably have one or two 'pensioners' among their stock, that is, one or two older dogs that have passed their breeding career and are now kept in retirement to live out their lives in the company of their caring owners.

At the other end of the scale are the people who use dogs as a means of making money. I include here puppy farmers, back-street breeders and other individuals whose only motive in keeping dogs is for the profits that they bring in. A typical example would be someone who owns two or more bitches which are little more than puppy-producing machines. The stud dog is selected only after cost comparisons have been made, with the cheapest dog being favoured. The bitches are never selected according to temperament and are rarely looked after correctly when in whelp (expecting puppies), while the puppies themselves are rarely given the best start in life and are sold to anyone who comes along with the required amount of money. Such breeders have only young breeding stock because they dispose of all dogs when they are no longer financially viable.

It is such a shame when dogs have to be kept in the manner of farm animals and valued in monetary terms rather than valued for the amount of enrichment that they can bring to our lives.

How much does your dog contribute to your life?

If you first of all decide why you want a dog in the first place and then take a closer look at the partnership, you should come up with a number of ways in which owning your dog enriches your life. The way to do this is to list all of the things that you and your family used to do in your leisure time before you obtained your dog. Write down a complete week's activities and include everything that you found enjoyable in your lifestyle in your pre-dog days. Then write down all of the things that you have done over the past week or so that you have found enjoyable. Now compare these two lists and you should find that your life has either remained unchanged or it has improved as a result of owning your dog. If, when comparing these lists, you find that your life has changed for the worse, then you must seriously question the reasons for getting a dog in the first place. You see, dogs do not simply fit into the gaps that we create in our lives, they have to be selected carefully so that the environment in which we are asking them to live is correct for their needs.

Let's take a look at a typical family and their lifestyle before the arrival of a pet dog.

Monday   Dad goes to work, children go to school, Mum goes to a coffee morning at a friend's house. No activity during the evening, the family sit and watch television and videos.

Tuesday   Shopping day for Mum, who goes into town with a friend for lunch. Evening activities include children's friends coming round to play and neighbours coming round for a social visit.

Wednesday   Friends call in to see Mum for a chat during the day. Evening activities often involve Dad and son going on a fishing trip to the local river and Mum and daughter going to the cinema.

Thursday   Mum helps out at the senior citizens' afternoon club. In the evening Dad goes to the local pub with friends leaving the rest of the family at home where Mum's friend comes visiting with her children.

Friday   Mum goes to keep fit class in the morning. The babysitter arrives in the evening to look after the children so that Mum and Dad can go out together for the evening.

Saturday   The family go on a shopping trip in the morning and have lunch out. In the afternoon the family go to the local beach for a walk and in the evening they usually attend a sporting event such as speedway racing or ice hockey.

Sunday   The morning is often spent gardening and in DIY activities. The family go to Grandma's for dinner and then

spend the rest of the afternoon socialising. Relations occasionally visit during the course of the evening.

Let's now go back and take a look at the same family several
months after the arrival of a new puppy.

Monday   Dad goes to work, children go to school, Mum takes
the dog to a coffee morning at a friend's house. The family take
the dog to the local dog-training club in the evening where they
meet and socialise with other dog owners.

Tuesday   Shopping day for Mum. After exercising the dog she
leaves it in the well-ventilated car while she shops and has
lunch with a friend. Evening activities remain unchanged.

Wednesday   Daytime activities unchanged, plus Mum meets
other dog owners while exercising the dog. The dog goes with
Dad and son fishing in the evening.

Thursday   The dog goes with Mum, much to the obvious
delight of the senior citizens who enjoy the company of man's
best friend. The evening remains unchanged.

Friday   Daytime remains unchanged, with the dog happy to
remain at home for a couple of hours while Mum goes out. The
evening remains unchanged.

Saturday   At the shops the children take it in turns to hold the
dog's lead when the rest of the family go into some shops. At
lunch-time the dog is put into the car for half an hour and settles
down to sleep. The dog is exercised on the beach all afternoon
and is left at home to sleep it off during the evening when the
family go out.

Sunday   The day proceeds as normal, with relatives enjoying
the company of a well-behaved dog.

So as you can see, the arrival of a dog has, if anything,
improved and enriched the lives of the family. They certainly
have not been prevented from doing anything now that they
have done in the past.

Let's now look at the same family several months after
buying the wrong dog for their needs and then bringing it up
badly without any formal education and believing that the dog
has an inbuilt sense of right and wrong.

Monday   Dad goes to work, the children go to school, Mum stays
at home because her friend will not allow the unruly dog into her
house. The dog's behaviour at the dog-training club is so bad that
in order to avoid further embarrassment they stop going.

Tuesday Shopping consists of a lightning visit with the dog being left barking at home because of the damage it does to the car if left. Lunch out is quite definitely out of the question. In the evening the children's friends can no longer visit because the dog cannot be trusted with them and, since the neighbours are growled at, they have stopped coming around.

Wednesday Friends no longer call and see Mum any more because of the dog's continuing aggression towards them. Exercising the dog in the local park is becoming a nightmare. In the evening either Mum and daughter or Dad and son must stay at home to look after the dog.

Thursday Mum no longer goes to the senior citizens' club because she cannot take the dog with her as it cannot be trusted with the elderly people, and she cannot leave it alone in the house because she would have no house to go back to: it chews. In the evening Mum sits alone in the house with the dog, the children go to their friends' house, Dad goes to the pub.

Friday Mum no longer goes anywhere because the dog has made her a prisoner in the house. The babysitter, after she was terrorised by the dog a few weeks ago, now refuses to come any more so Mum and Dad take it in turns to have a night out.

Saturday Mum takes the children to the shops and for lunch, leaving Dad at home to look after the dog. Dad takes the children to the beach while Mum looks after the dog. Saturday nights out are a thing of the past.

Sunday There is very little left of what once used to be the garden as the dog has dug holes in the lawn and pulled out most of the plants. Grandma will not allow the dog into her house and so only half the family visit each week. Relations have stopped visiting.

It does not take me to point out that, since buying a dog, this family's life has been ruined. The dog in question is based on one of the many 'problem' dogs that I come across each week. What will surprise you is that the actual dog described above was not a Dobermann or a Rottweiler but a Yorkshire Terrier!

A small amount of thought before buying a dog can usually save years and years of torment for owners and public alike, but sadly far too many puppies are purchased on impulse by well-meaning people only to be given a life of constant mental cruelty. So what sort of life would a pet dog want for itself if it had the choice in terms of exercise, attention, affection, feeding, grooming, sleeping and training? The answer to most of these questions is, of course, going to depend largely on the breed of dog and so it is from that standpoint that we will examine them more closely.

Physical exercise

Almost all dogs benefit from daily sessions of free running exercise during which time they can expend some energy by using all of the muscle groups that nature has given them. The breeds of dog in the working category need by far the largest area for free exercise, while many of the toy breeds can be adequately exercised in a very small area. Walking a dog on a lead and denying it the right to exercise freely is just plain cruelty and there is never any excuse for subjecting a dog to mental cruelty. So when you select a dog of a particular breed, consider the size of your garden and take note of any local by laws which may prohibit free exercise in public places.

Attention and affection

Part of the reasons behind people owning pet dogs is the desire to give attention and show affection towards another living creature. As long as rules are established regarding the terms under which the dog gains attention, then the dog should never become a nuisance to the point where it starts to pester the owner or worse still to misbehave in order to gain attention. It should therefore be the owner who instigates the majority of the attention and affection that the young dog receives (see Chapter 3, Surviving the First Six Months).

Our desire to own companion dogs is based largely on our desire to maintain a close contact with nature because it makes us feel more relaxed. It is for this reason, so I am told, that we keep houseplants and arrange to take holidays in the country and near to water – this awakens our ancestral links with the world of nature. The dog, unlike our houseplants, is capable of returning all the affection and attention that we bestow upon it many times over.

The Parliament of Monaco has recently passed a law which states that 'the animal is a sensitive being that must be respected, cared for and protected'. It prohibits companion animals from upsetting others by their behaviour; sets up education programmes in schools; gives tenants the right to keep a companion animal in rented housing, and obliges homes for the elderly to accept the animals of their residents.

Her Supreme Highness Princess Antoinette of Monaco said in a speech, 'since my childhood I have been deeply marked by the affectionate presence of animals', and she went on to remark on the last provision of the new law by saying that 'because of the deep distress of some elderly persons, often abandoned by their children and their dear ones, the companion animal is their last resort, their ultimate joy, their final confidante and their last stimulus'.

Feeding

It is important that your dog receives a regular and correctly balanced diet to maintain an active and healthy life. With modern convenience foods it is quick and easy to prepare your dog's meals in the knowledge that it will be receiving the balance of protein, carbohydrates, vitamins, minerals and trace elements necessary for its well being. The only problem is that because the pet-food industry is concerned with selling their products, they strive to make them more and more appetising with the end result that a great number of dogs eat far more than they need to in order to survive and so tend to put on weight. A large proportion of pet dogs that I see are overweight, with some of them grossly overweight. There is also the tendency of late to give dogs vitamin and mineral supplements believing that it will result in a stronger, healthier animal, with the result that large numbers of dogs receive overdoses of supplements. If your dog is fed a balanced, manufactured diet it is totally unnecessary to give food supplements unless advised to do so by your vet. Manufacturers spend thousands of pounds to ensure that their feedstuffs contain all that is nutritionally necessary for your dog's well being, so make sure that you read the directions that are supplied as a guide to feeding and if in doubt, consult your vet who will be happy to advise you.

Grooming

For your dog's coat to remain in good condition and to ensure that you detect any skin problems or parasitic infestations at the earliest possible stage, it is important to groom your dog on a regular basis. The frequency of grooming will be largely dependent on the length and type of your dog's coat. It is essential that short-coated breeds are groomed on a regular basis initially to accustom them to being handled as described in Chapter 3, Surviving the First Six Months.

Sleeping

Your dog should be provided with a safe and comfortable sleeping area out of damp or draughts. If you own one of the short-coated breeds then you will have to make provision for some form of heating during the winter months. However temperature and light are considered to be controlling influences on coat shedding, and so long-coated breeds are really better off if they have an unheated sleeping area. The coat remains in better condition and hairs are shed only twice each year instead of the all-year-round moulting that is associated with long-coated dogs kept in centrally heated environments. The dog's sleeping area should be positioned so that it is in a quiet area away from general household traffic but nevertheless in a position that is accessible to the owners so that it does not believe that it has the sole and exclusive right to be in that particular spot.

Training

Formal training should be carried out consistently by everyone in the family so that the dog learns that the same rules apply irrespective of who is around at the time. It is unfair to expect the dog to obey everyone that gives it instructions if only one person has bothered to carry out the training. Guide dogs, police dogs, search dogs, etc. are all trained by experienced and skilful handlers, and the same skills can be available to you and your family at a good dog-training club and from books in your local library.

Please remember that not all dog training clubs are good ones. You should attend without taking your dog on the first occasion to watch how the training is carried out and the effect on the dogs taking part.

2

Selecting a Puppy

Anyone having bred a litter of puppies from their pet bitch can, I suppose, be loosely termed a breeder and so the potential buyer needs to exercise caution so as to avoid problems and disappointment in the weeks and months to follow the purchase of a new puppy. There are many motives for people breeding litters of puppies and so it may be worthwhile examining the reasons that lie behind breeders producing puppies. Firstly we have the pet owner who wants just one litter of puppies from the bitch, believing that it will improve her temperament or 'calm her down'. In almost all cases, however, breeding a litter from a bitch with a poor temperament will serve only to compound any problems already present. If, for instance, you are having problems with your bitch being possessive or territorial, then the arrival of a litter of puppies will dramatically increase any aggressive tendencies towards owners and visitors. Give a protective bitch something 'special' to protect like pups of her own and she will protect them with great vigour! It also goes without saying, I hope, that *we should not be breeding puppies from bitches with suspect temperaments* as we will only be perpetuating problems.

Occasionally a litter is produced when the owner has a dog and a bitch. Because the male is continually mounting the owner's leg, other dogs, etc., he is used at stud in the mistaken belief that he 'needs a bitch' as he is starting to show signs of maturity. A bitch is, in fact, the last thing that he needs; castration would be far more appropriate in terms of improving his anti-social behaviour. Mating a bitch will make the over-sexed dog's behaviour worse and not better.

Some breeders produce puppies purely for financial gain, caring little about either the quality of offspring or the subsequent homes into which they are to be placed. Providing the buyer turns up with the required amount of money he or she is guaranteed a puppy with no questions asked. As different breeds become popular and the fashions change, so our profit-seeking breeder will change his breeding stock in order to satisfy the inevitable demand for puppies. This type of individual has been responsible for the downfall of many breeds, such as Golden Cocker Spaniels, German Shepherds, Dobermanns and more recently Rottweilers, with all of the caring, responsible breeders being left to pick up the pieces.

There are many, many people who simply see breeding as a means of supplementing their income or even being their main source of finance. Take, for instance, a person owning two Rottweiler bitches back in 1988 at the height of the breed's popularity. Breeding two litters of puppies from each bitch per year with an average of eight puppies per litter gives thirty-two pups which, selling at an average of £250 each, gives the breeder an annual income of £8000! Then as the popularity of the breed starts to decline, this 'breeder' sells off his brood bitches and invests in two or three Japanese Akita bitches, anticipating the next breed to be in demand.

Always go to the breeders who have built up a reputation for the quality of stock that they produce for both temperament and type. A really good breeder will usually have a waiting list and will want to talk to you at length before adding your name to that list. Remember, they have a reputation to protect and will not place their name in jeopardy by selling pups to anyone that may come along with a pocket full of money.

Remember that an initial interview is a two-way process. It allows the breeder to decide whether you are able to provide the correct sort of environment in which to bring up a puppy, and it is also an opportunity for you to ask questions and decide if the breed and breeding are what you really want. Dependent on the breed you select, owning a dog is a ten-to-fifteen-year commitment and it is wise to take plenty of time before coming to a decision.

To help you to make up your mind about the motives of the breeder, the following questions may be helpful.

Ask why the litter was bred. If the answer is to improve the temperament of the bitch, don't buy the puppy – there is a real danger that, like mum, the puppy will have a poor temperament. Ask how long the 'breeder' has owned that particular breed and how many dogs they have had. If they have only ever owned one dog of the breed, tread cautiously as they are likely to have little or no knowledge of the breed's characteristics.

Ask to see the breeder's old dogs – if they do not have any then do not purchase a puppy from them. Caring, responsible breeders will have been involved in dogs for a number of years and will almost certainly have older dogs that have passed their prime and are now being kept in retirement to live out their lives in comfort. If the so-called breeder does not have any old dogs it could well be the case that his older dogs are sold off as their useful profit-making, breeding days are over.

Ask to see their Breeder's Licence. The Breeding of Dogs Act (1973) requires that anyone owning more than two bitches for the purposes of breeding should be licensed by the local authority which sets out a number of minimum requirements that the breeder must comply with in order to obtain the licence. Most of the requirements are designed to ensure the welfare of bitches and puppies. Only reputable breeders will have such a licence; most 'casual' breeders will not even have heard about the Breeder's Licence.

Most good breeders will offer to take back and re-home any puppy they sell which proves to be unsuitable, in order to maintain their reputation; a casual breeder will not.

You would also be well advised not to purchase a puppy which was not bred on the premises as you will be unable to see the mother. Puppy farms which buy in litters of puppies for re-sale are exempt from the Breeder's Licence as the puppies are not actually being bred but simply bought and sold. The kennel or pet shop is then acting simply as a dealer and is rarely interested in the subsequent home that the puppies go into. The aim of puppy farms and dealers is to buy litters of pups as cheaply as possible, sell them as quickly as possible and make the maximum profit. A look at the conditions in which the puppies are kept will confirm that the dealer does not exactly have the puppies' welfare at heart. A list of breeders may be obtained by contacting the Kennel Club or the secretary of the breed society of the breed you are interested in. Purchasing one of the many canine periodicals will greatly assist in locating a breeder.

The stud dog

It would be fairly rare for the father of the puppies to be available for inspection on the premises but if the breeder does, in fact, own the stud dog it would be well worth asking to see him first to get some idea of his likely temperament. It would be fairly unlikely for a reputable breeder to use anything other than a stud dog of outstanding temperament and so it would rarely be worthwhile to travel any great distance to see the father. Besides which, even though there is obviously a genetic factor involved in temperament, by far the greatest influence on the puppies' future behaviour is environmental. If the father is of a nervous disposition and has been allowed a great deal of access to his puppies, they may well start to copy his nervous behaviour when placed under stress.

We'll now take a look at mum away from her puppies. Ask for her to be brought into the house if she is normally kept in a kennel. Watch her behaviour closely. Is she friendly? Is the breeder confident enough to allow her to come in unrestrained by collar and lead? Does the breeder seem apprehensive about the way the bitch approaches you? Can you touch and stroke the bitch? The obvious ones to avoid are bitches that either have to be restrained, come in barking and are reluctant to stop, or are unapproachable. If the bitch exhibits any of the above behaviour, I would not bother even to see the puppies. I know that anyone with a little patience and a lot of under-standing of the canine mind could easily purchase a puppy from such a bitch and end up with a perfectly well-behaved adult dog. It is, however, inadvisable to attempt to bring up a puppy of dubious temperament unless you have the necessary expertise. It is nearly always doomed to failure as the majority of puppies mimic the behaviour of their mothers. If all goes well at this stage then ask to be taken to where the puppies are normally kept. Don't have them brought in to meet you – that comes later. Entering the room or kennel where the puppies are, let the bitch enter with you, free of any restraint. The bitch's behaviour should not change towards you at all; she should remain friendly and confident. Now observe the behaviour of the puppies. Stand still and some of the bolder ones should approach, encouraged by the entrance of their mother. For a good pet dog, discount any of the over-bold, pushy puppies. These are often referred to as the troublemakers or dominant ones and may prove to be a little too headstrong for an average owner who simply wants a well-behaved pet. If you are looking for a dog as a dual-purpose pet/working dog to enter any of the various forms of canine competitions and are able to devote a lot of time in education, then a more dominant pup may be the wisest choice. The pup that sits in the corner and will not approach, even when you are stroking mum and the other pups are pushing for attention, should also be discarded as a prospective family pet.

A pup that is slow to approach and then as it gets near, starts to crawl on its belly or when you touch it or stroke it, and rolls over to expose its underparts would normally make a reasonable pet dog as it is likely to remain submissive throughout its life and would rarely cause problems. It is important not to confuse submission with nervousness. A submissive puppy shows no signs of fear and would not avoid contact.

Again it should go without saying that if, when you are taken in to see the puppies, the bitch starts to become agitated or aggressive, then discount all of the puppies! If the puppies will not approach you, remaining huddled together and seeming uneasy about your presence, then be very cautious about purchasing any. It is probably the case that they have had little or no social contact with people.

Once you have decided whether it is to be a dog or a bitch that you want, ask the breeder to separate them into sexes and take the pups of the sex of your choice into the house or part of the house away from mum and the rest of the litter. If you observe the behaviour of the pups away from the influence of mum and the other pups and away from their familiar surroundings you will get a clearer picture as to which are dominant, as these will be the first to explore the new surroundings. If all the pups huddle together and refuse to move, suspect that they have never been socialised or seen any environment other than that in which they were born, the breeder has never had them in a family environment, making subsequent re-homing more difficult and possibly more traumatic. The pups that cry and howl for their mother and litter-mates are going to lead to a great deal of sleepless nights at the outset. The pups who show little or no change in behaviour from their familiar surroundings will be comparatively easy to integrate into a new family environment. Ideally the breeder should have seen to it that all of the puppies have been well handled and introduced to normal household sounds; the pups should enjoy being touched and should not cringe at human contact, and neither should they be bothered about being spoken to.

Having made a choice, based if possible on at least two separate visits, a few days apart, you will be given lots of information by the breeder. If in fact you class yourself as a breeder then the following list may prove useful to ensure that new owners leave you with all the information they require to ensure the best possible start in life for their chosen puppy.

1. *Vaccination* – The breeder should explain about recommended vaccines suitable to give a degree of protection against all of the major canine diseases. New vaccines are being continually developed to give greater protection at an earlier age than in previous years and good breeders usually have a rapport with their veterinary practices and have a layman's knowledge of such matters. The breeder should also give you the timing of such vaccination procedures.

2. *Worming* – All puppies are born with roundworms and the breeder should already have taken steps to ensure that the puppies are clear of worms when sold, but should also explain the necessity of worming the pup again at intervals to prevent re-infestation. The roundworm (*Toxicara canis*) has been the focus of adverse publicity surrounding dogs because of the danger of ingestion where children have access to play areas where dogs are allowed to foul. The simple answer to the problem is to ensure that every dog owner worms their dog on a regular basis – end of problem!

3. *Registration with the Kennel Club (if applicable)* – The breeder should give you all the papers to enable you to transfer the pup's registration to your name. It is now only the breeder who can register the puppy with the Kennel Club. Details concerning registration can be obtained from the Kennel Club, 1 Clarges Street, Piccadilly, London W1Y 8AB enclosing a large stamped addressed envelope.

You should also be given a copy of the puppy's pedigree, which may well be meaningless to you and so ask the breeder to explain what it all means. The length of the dog's pedigree is totally irrelevant to the quality of the puppy and is dictated only by the breeder's desire to carry out a large amount of writing. Remember that anyone can go into a pet shop and purchase pedigree forms and can then write anything on them that takes their fancy. It is in fact possible to write out a pedigree for a mongrel; a pedigree is simply a list of ancestors laid out as a family tree on a piece of paper.

4. *Diet* – You should be given a comprehensive diet sheet which details type of food recommended, frequency of feeding, amounts, etc. You will then either be given or will be asked to purchase a small supply of food that the puppies have been fed on by the breeder. If you wish to change the basic diet at any stage of the pup's life you should do so gradually to avoid tummy upsets. It is vital that for at least the first week of life in its new family environment, the pup is fed in terms identical to that which existed with the breeder. If you always make a point of reading the dog-food manufacturer's recommendations you cannot really go far wrong.

5. *Insurance* – Most breeders will insure their puppies against illness or accident and this insurance cover will usually still be operative when you buy a puppy. You are normally given the option of taking out your own insurance policy on your puppy which, in addition to paying vets' fees in the event of ill health, will often reimburse the consultation fee of a dog-behaviour consultant if problems arise later in the pup's life, providing it is on veterinary referral.

6. *Grooming/handling* – Breeders of long-coated breeds such as Afghan Hounds or Bearded Collies will usually take the time and trouble to explain to the new owner how to groom the puppy all over to ensure that the coat remains in good condition, free of mats and tangles. This is often carried out using an older dog to demonstrate on, followed by carrying out the same process on the puppy that is about to be purchased. This ensures that the new owners groom and handle the dog daily, which is not only necessary for the dog's coat but it also gets the young puppy used to being restrained and handled on

the owner's terms. Sadly, most breeders who specialise in short-coated breeds such as Rottweilers, Dobermanns and Labradors, etc. never explain the importance of daily grooming/handling lessons with the young puppy. The result is that, because the dog has never learnt to be restrained while it was a puppy, it becomes increasingly difficult for anyone such as the vet, training instructor, or even the owner to touch it on their terms. A fully grown Dobermann that has never allowed its owners to groom it all over without a real struggle is not going to take kindly to a vet trying to examine a sore ear!

So regardless of the breed you are selecting, ask the breeder to show you how to groom and handle the puppy you are about to purchase. This more than anything else will show you just how well the puppies have been handled. If the puppy becomes hysterical or aggressive with the breeder, *do not buy that puppy*. As I have said before, an experienced owner may, with patience and understanding, improve the puppy in a short space of time, but why start off with problems? If the puppy accepts the grooming process, ask to have a go yourself. It is a fair bet that if the breeder had no problems, neither will you, and providing that you continue the process, neither will your friends, the vet, the training instructor, the judge, etc.

7. *Socialisation* – Try to find out the extent of any socialisation that has already taken place, even though this will of necessity, because of the risk of infection, etc., have been limited. Has the puppy had contact with people other than the breeders (male or female)? Has the puppy met children or dogs other than its mother? Has it been confined to a kennel for the majority of its life or has it spent some or even all of its life in a household environment? This will at least give you some idea as to where to start with your own socialisation programme.

Having gone through one or two litter inspections and asked a number of questions, you should now be in a position to make a choice between the puppies, and even though things can still go wrong when the pup arrives in a new environment to start its life as a family dog, you have at least reduced the possibility of problems down to a minimum.

The last thing that you should ask the breeder to do for you in order to help your puppy settle into your house with the minimum of upset is this. Two days before you pick up your puppy ask for a piece of warm material, about one square metre, to be placed in the box where the puppies sleep. It should be left in place until you arrive to collect your chosen pup. It should then be removed and placed inside a polythene bag, sealed and handed to you when you leave for home. It is extremely important for both you and the puppy (and your neighbours) that you have this piece of material when you arrive home. The reason will become clear in the next chapter – Surviving the First Six Months.

3

Surviving the First Six Months

Having arrived home with your new puppy, the responsibility for its future health, physical and mental well being and behaviour rests firmly on your shoulders. It's of little use blaming the breeder for anything other than hereditary defects in the areas that they have some control over, such as conformation, etc. Formal education and continued socialisation are now your concern and undoubtedly the greatest influence on the developing pup's behaviour is the effect of its environment, particularly up to sixteen weeks of age but continuing, to a lesser extent, up to maturity. Thus, a dog that is brought up in a country environment, away from traffic, other dogs and children, would have great difficulty in adjusting to a move to a busy town, where it would be expected to exercise and mix with other dogs and children.

So the first six months are concerned with laying down the foundations of acceptable behaviour and educating the young dog in a way that puts the owners gently but firmly in control.

Games and play

Almost every puppy plays games, the only exception being single surviving pups or occasionally pups that have had their play instinct suppressed by an over-dominant mother. Play serves many purposes in young animals, the primary purpose being to improve co-ordination and skills necessary for future survival. If you either fail to provide an outlet for the creative, enquiring pup's mind or over-stimulate it during play sessions you could easily end up with problems as it grows and matures, so it is as well to put a little thought into the games that you and the family play.

Toys

The idea behind providing your puppy with toys is to allow you to build up a relationship with it using a common interest through play. There is a terrific variety of toys on the market designed to stimulate your pup's interest in playing games, but the toys themselves can be made even more enjoyable if you provide lots of movement and excitement. A toy that remains immobile will do little to stimulate a young dog into playing with it. We can roughly divide games into three main types:

1. *Killing games* – Usually played with a squeaky toy or a piece of rag. The idea is that the dog crushes the toy again and again in its jaws while shaking it violently from side to side. This duplicates the action of killing a live prey. The dog crushes with its jaws and the toy squeals; the shaking is designed to bring down a large animal or break the back of a smaller one. This is why dogs that become over-excited when they play with squeaky toys tend to chew them and then lose interest when the toy is dead, i.e. the squeaker no longer works.

Typical killing (squeaky) toys

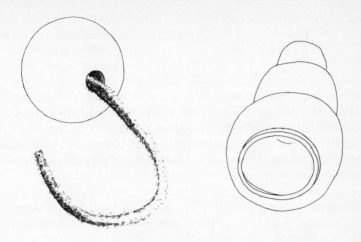

Typical chasing toys – ball on a rope and Kong toy

2. *Chasing games* – Often played with a ball, which is a particularly good toy for this game as, unlike most other toys it will continue to roll along the ground after it lands, thereby exciting the dog's instinct to chase. It is the movement that makes it attractive. Hold on to a puppy and roll a ball, releasing it only when the ball has come to rest for a few seconds, and the pup would be unlikely to show anywhere near the interest that it would show if it were released while the ball was moving.

3. *Possession games* – Usually played with rubber rings or pull toys, the idea being a game of strength or tug-of-war during

Typical possession (tug-of-war) toys

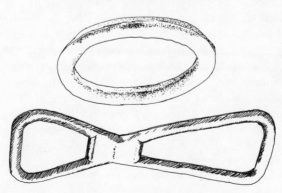

which dog and owner pit their physical strength against one another, the ultimate victor being the stronger and often the more dominant. Prising a possession toy out of a dominant dog's mouth is usually quite difficult as the more the owner pulls, the harder the dog pulls and fights to retain possession. Playful growling often accompanies the game, with the owner mimicking the growling noises made by the puppy. Winning the game even for a few seconds is difficult enough, but trying to hold on to the toy and prevent the pup from touching it again until you invite it to usually results in the pup getting more and more agitated.

Frequently puppies will play all three games, but there is always one favourite game that it will play longer and more enthusiastically than either of the other two. This is due mainly to selective breeding to produce dogs to fulfil a particular purpose. Terriers have been selectively bred to produce dogs that have had their killing instinct exaggerated. Sheepdogs have evolved mainly as chasing dogs, while guard dogs are generally the ones that have evolved as being extremely possessive.

So you see that the games that your puppy plays are very important and a large number of behaviour problems present in adult dogs may be traced back to games that they played as puppies.

Games should be mentally stimulating as well as requiring modest amounts of physical exertion on the part of the puppy. One of the most useful games to play is retrieving and when the pup starts to understand what is required, the search exercise can be incorporated into the basic retrieve. Most pups will be interested in running after a thrown toy, preferably after a small amount of teasing on the part of the owner and providing the toy continues to move as the pup runs after it. Most pups will attempt to pick it up and then take it to a 'safe' place to investigate it further or to chew it. Most owners immediately intervene by walking over to where the pup has taken the toy and removing it from the pup's mouth before repeating the teasing/throwing process. In a fairly short time the pup learns to avoid the owner's attempts to steal the toy and far from retrieving it, will actually run away from the owner with it. To prevent this happening simply tease the pup with the toy and then throw it, encouraging the pup to chase it. When it picks up the toy, do not give chase. Allow the pup to take the toy anywhere it wants to. When it settles down with the toy, by the side of the coffee table for instance, quietly walk over and sit alongside. Stroke the pup while it is investigating and chewing the toy. If at any time the pup drops the toy or relinquishes it, praise really well before picking up the toy and returning to the exact spot from where the toy was thrown initially. Tease the pup with the toy and then repeat.

After four or five repetitions of the above, you should find, regardless of the direction in which you throw the toy, the pup always returns to the same spot with it to lie down and chew it. All you need to do now is throw the toy and while the pup is running after it, quickly go and sit in the spot you know the puppy will head for. Sit there quietly as the pup approaches and when it lies down, stroke it gently and praise it. Do not attempt to take the toy from the pup unless it drops it by itself or until the pup has played with it for a couple of minutes. You must not lead the pup to believe that you are entering into a competition for possession of the toy. Once you have the toy then throw it again from the position you are in.

If all goes well the pup should immediately go to pick it up and return to you. Repeat the stroking/praising before obtaining the toy once more. If the pup does not release the toy of its

Removing a toy from a
puppy's mouth

own free will, then gently stroke its head and then place your finger and thumb into its mouth on each side just behind the toy. Its mouth should then open and the toy will drop out (see illustration). Never try to pull the toy out as the pup may only grip harder and then see the whole game as a competition of strength and start teasing you with the toy by staying out of arm's reach. Always stop playing before the pup gets bored with the game and remember to put that particular toy away so that it remains 'special' to this game. The next few times that you play this game remember to position yourself in the place you know the puppy will head for when it picks up the thrown toy. After a few such sessions, try moving your position. If all goes well then the pup should always head towards you with the toy in anticipation of the pleasant association of being praised and stroked.

If, on the other hand, the pup does not come towards you but goes back to its familar position, try tapping your fingertips on the floor. This should create enough interest to encourage the pup to investigate the drumming noise and with luck it should come towards you with the toy; praise well and stroke when it does so. If it drops the toy when it comes to you, still praise well and stroke because at least the pup has got a part of the action that you require correct. It would help if you could move any furniture or rugs from the old location to your new position. Holding on to the pup, pick up the toy and throw it back near the position where it had been dropped. Repeat in short sessions until you get the response you require.

The vast majority of dog owners teach their puppies the exact opposite of a retrieve by throwing a toy and then when the pup picks it up, chasing it around before snatching the toy away. The end result is that the pup either refuses to play, knowing it cannot compete with its owner, and will therefore stand back and watch the toy being thrown and then expect the owner to retrieve it, or will race after the toy and take every avoiding action necessary to stop the owner from getting it.

Extending the basic retrieve into the more mentally demanding search exercise is detailed fully in my previous book, *Your Dog: Its Development, Behaviour and Training*.

Squeaky toys, particularly for the terrier breeds, can be made a great deal more exciting by first of all attaching a length of string to the toy and pulling it around the floor for the pup to chase after. Remember not to get the pup overtired by making it run too far before allowing it to catch and kill the toy. Because the toy is on a length of string it is easy to prevent the dog from chewing it up and destroying it. After a few sessions of teaching the pup to play the game of chase and kill, you can introduce a new element to the game which will provide more mental stimulation. Obtain a two- to three-foot length of plastic drainpipe and select a squeaky toy that will fit easily inside it. Now fasten a length of string to either end of the toy and, after first teasing the pup, place it in the pipe with the string protruding from each end of the pipe.

If you now pull on one string, the toy will emerge from that end of the pipe. As the pup goes to pick it up, pull the other string and the toy will vanish back into the pipe. Wait for a few seconds and then pull either string to make the toy emerge. Allow the pup to kill it for a minute or so and then repeat. To start with, allow the pup to get the toy once for every twice you make it emerge from either end of the pipe and keep it waiting for only a few seconds. As its concentration improves you can increase the waiting time to two minutes until the toy appears at random, from either end of the tube. You can also carefully decrease the frequency of times the pup is allowed actually to kill the toy down to about one in five.

Making games more exciting by utilising a basic toy and some additional 'props'

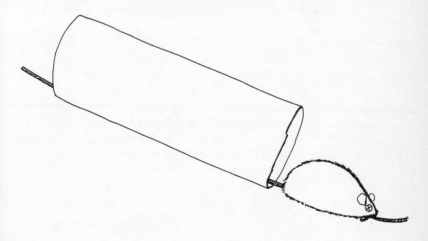

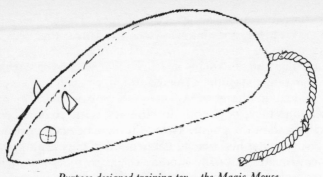

Purpose designed training toy – the Magic Mouse

Remember not to overdo these play sessions. Always stop before the pup gets tired and put the toys away.

Games of tug-of-war are potentially the most dangerous games for owners to play with their puppy because if the dog starts to win and control these games, as it may have done with its litter-mates, it can easily grow up thinking it is stronger and more dominant than the family it lives with. It is therefore extremely important that games of tug end up with the owners winning more times than the pup and ultimately with the toy being taken away and put where the puppy has no access to it, until required for the next play session. To play the game of tug, hold the toy in your hand and wave it from side to side until the pup grips it. Then start to make a few gentle thrusting

Professionally designed play equipment. The Flymouse Machine is designed to throw a furry magic mouse for the dog to catch when it operates the pedal with its paw

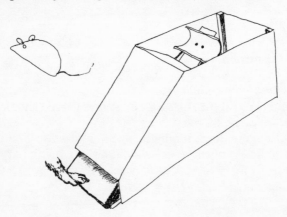

movements, towards then away from him. This should make him grip tighter and mimic the movements that you are producing.

If, during the game, the pup starts to growl, even if it sounds playful, quickly stop the game by removing the toy (see page 39–40) and at the same time saying 'leave' or 'drop'. Wait for a few minutes to allow the pup to calm and settle before playing again. We want the pup to learn that under no circumstances must he growl at his owners, particularly if they are trying to remove something from his mouth. To ensure that the pup does not tire of always losing the game of tug, it is quite a good idea to allow it to win, temporarily, about once in every four or five times it is invited to play, but even this has to be controlled. The danger is that while you are tugging, if you occasionally release your grip, the pup will run off with the toy and try to prevent you from getting it again. To counter this tendency simply put a puppy collar on the pup and attach a six-foot length of light cord. When you release your grip on the toy, if there is a tendency for the pup to try to avoid your outstretched hand, simply pick up the line and insist that the dog returns to give its toy back to you. Once the puppy has learned to play the game and also understands that you are stronger than he is, you can progress to throwing the toy a short distance, again using the line if necessary, and get him to retrieve it in order to play tug-of-war. Once that has been mastered you can teach the pup to search for a concealed toy in order to retrieve and play tug.

Controlling the games

One of the main educational aspects of all play sessions should be the controlling influence of the owner. That means the owner and not the puppy should decide when a game should start, how long it should go on for and, more importantly, when it should end. All the rules for any games played should also be set, very clearly, by the owner.

Just imagine, for a moment, owning an adult dog that has learnt to dictate when it will play, how long it will play for and when the game must end, and has also learnt to set all the rules regarding play. When visitors arrive and the dog gets excited, it decides to play. The game includes jumping up and down tugging at the visitor's jacket sleeves, trouser legs, etc. and the owners are powerless to stop it because it has never been taught any form of control while playing. Contrast that with a puppy which has been taught that play sessions occur when its owners invite a game with a favourite toy by producing that toy from a cupboard. During the game the owners dictate how the puppy is allowed to play, i.e. no growling or putting its teeth on any part of the owner's clothing and no jumping up. The game finishes when the owners tell the pup, 'that's enough' or 'finish' and immediately put the toy away in a position where the pup has no access to it. With this puppy, as it matures into an adult dog, the owners are in the perfect position to control any games that the dog tries to play with visitors as it has already learnt that its owners are in control of any games.

So how is this sort of control achieved? Well, to start with it is better that all toys are kept under the control of the owner in a position where the pup has no unsupervised access to them. It now becomes even more important that the puppy has several daily play sessions or it will go looking for toys and mischief on its own! Produce a toy preferably as a reward for any sort of behaviour that you want to encourage, i.e. going into the garden and relieving itself or coming in response to its name. During the game make sure that what the pup does is acceptable to you – that is, if you throw the toy teach the pup to bring it back; if it tugs the toy with you, teach it to release immediately it is told; if it tries to tear the toy to pieces, teach it not to. Play for as long as you want, always making sure that the game ends before the pup gets bored. Teach it the command 'enough' or 'finished' when you end the game by putting the toy away. Ignore any attempts that the puppy may make in order to get you to continue the game. When the pup has accepted that the game is over, give it a large hide chew or marrowbone to amuse itself with, which it can do quite happily without the owner needing to participate.

Over-stimulation

Play that over-stimulates a young dog will invariably cause problems for the owner later when the dog turns a simple game into an obsession which gets completely beyond control. One example would be the owners encouraging a very young pup to bark when the doorbell rings. They even purposely go and stand at the door and sound the bell several times each day to watch the pup race to the door and bark. By the time the puppy reaches the age of eighteen months, when its natural guarding instincts would have started to develop anyway, the owners have a dog that barks furiously and races back and forth not only when anyone rings the doorbell but also when anyone walks past the house. The poor owners are powerless to do anything about the dog's behaviour and it has now become a problem dog.

If you go to any dog-training club you will doubtless see dogs, particularly sheepdogs, that have been over-stimulated in games of chase. As puppies their owners would have encouraged them to chase and retrieve all sorts of toys after first teasing them furiously. No control of the chase aspect of the game was ever taught, the only education that the dog ever received being the actual bringing it back to the owner. The end result is that these dogs get over-excited by quick, sudden movements, particularly when a retrieve exercise is taking place in the dog-club hall and nothing the owners do can stop them barking hysterically and straining at the lead when a dumb-bell is thrown. Or how about a pup that the owners have encouraged to pull on a toy, or even their sleeves, and have encouraged to growl louder and louder and pull harder and harder to the point where the pup has become out of control or 'lost its temper'. The game ends when the owner relinquishes possession of the toy to the pup or the pup bites the owner harder and harder until it draws blood. By the time this pup is a year old it will have learnt to use aggression, i.e. baring its teeth, growling and biting to win any encounter with its owners, and will possibly go for the arm of anyone it feels is threatening.

To avoid problems in later life you must ensure that games never get out of hand to the point where a simple game or part of a game becomes an obsession on the dog's part. This is where some simple do's and don'ts may prove useful:

DO spend as much time playing with your puppy (and your adult dog) as you can.

DO encourage other people to play with your pup using the same rules and toys as you use.

DO add variety and extend the concentration required by the pup during the games.

DO pick the type of toy and the type of game that most interests your puppy.

DO use toys and games to reward good behaviour.

DO use toys to train your puppy formally to come when called, sit, etc. as a reward for obeying in the same way that you would use food (titbits).

DON'T allow anyone to play games that involve too much teasing which promises the reward of a toy but rarely produces the reward.

DON'T allow the pup to put its teeth on any part of your body in play. It can put its teeth on, and, if necessary, learn to inhibit its bite (gundogs) on a toy.

DON'T allow the pup to growl at you in play.

DON'T allow the pup to become over-excited or hysterical during a game. Call a 'time out' or stop the game completely.

DON'T allow the pup to play games that your friends, neighbours or members of the general public would find annoying.

DON'T allow the pup to use you as it would a toy.

DON'T play wrestling games on the floor, particularly if you own one of the larger breeds.

The following are suggestions to prevent a puppy from becoming obsessed with aspects of play when it shows signs of becoming over-excited.

Chase games with a toy – occasionally hold on to the puppy and throw the toy, keeping it restrained and thus preventing it from running after the toy until it loses interest. Then go and pick up the toy yourself and encourage the pup to chase and retrieve it next time it is thrown. If you do this at random about once every ten times the toy is thrown, you will teach the pup that it is not allowed to run and chase everything that moves.

To improve control further you can teach the chase recall. With a young puppy all it takes is to throw the toy towards another person, and when the pup runs towards the toy, call it back when about half-way there. As you call, have the other person quickly pick up the toy to prevent the pup from reaching it. When it turns to come back, throw a second toy in the opposite direction to the first toy. Carried out correctly the pup will become more and more responsive to being called back when it sets out to chase anything. The advantages of a dog that will first of all not chase unless allowed to do so and, even when chasing anything, will return instantly should be obvious to all dog owners. Remember that you are simply trying to establish some measure of control during games. Do not overdo this control or you may reduce the pup's desire to play the game.

Tugging games – whenever the puppy starts to show signs of becoming out of control when tugging, quickly remove the toy from its mouth (see page 39–40). The trick now is to hold the toy within the dog's reach but do not allow it to touch the toy, using the same technique as you used to remove it, i.e. hold your finger and thumb close to the toy ready to prevent the pup from actually taking hold. If the pup then prefers playing games of biting the offending fingers that are preventing him from touching the toy, put something that tastes unpleasant on your fingers such as Bitter Apple. When the pup accepts that it can no longer get the toy and gives up all attempts to regain possession, praise well and invite it to play again. When you get to the stage where, when you say 'leave' the pup releases its grip

Preventing a dog from returning to touch the toy until it is invited to by the owner

and stands back waiting for your invitation to recommence play, you can teach it to sit or lie down for a few seconds before restarting the game. Carried out correctly you should end up with a dog that will only ever put its teeth on a toy, and at any time the toy is produced will instantly be under the control of its owner.

Killing games – these games actually get out of control only on rare occasions, the reason being that when puppies start to become obsessed with killing and destroying squeaky toys (designed to produce a squeal and effect similar to that made by a small animal being killed by a dog) the owner stops buying them because of the expense. The dog then has its killing instinct suppressed to a degree by having access only to less effective toys in terms of continuing its obsession with killing.

To ensure that killing games do not get out of hand, always ensure that the puppy does not get carried away in play to the point where it starts to tear up the toy. This is most easily accomplished using the piece of string mentioned earlier. What you should do is quickly to use the string to remove the toy the minute the pup starts to kill it for real. Allow it to squeak it, toss it around and pounce on it, but no more. Use a command of 'leave' each time you recover the toy, and wait for the pup to settle and calm down before recommencing the game. Carried out correctly you will have conditioned the dog to play a toned-down version of killing games and also made it fairly gentle-mouthed into the bargain.

Play environment

In addition to playing with the puppy and ensuring that you are in control of the games, it is important that the puppy learns to play in different environments.

If, for example, you play with your puppy in the living room for the first two weeks, you shouldn't expect the pup to play the same games, with the same amount of enthusiasm, if you go into your dining room or your friend's living room to play.

Some dogs grow up learning to play only in their own homes and refuse to play outside, whereas some will play only outside in the local park and will not play in the house. The trick with a young pup is, when you have got it to enjoy playing games in one room go into another and repeat the game. If the pup is reluctant to play in that environment, stop playing all games in the first room and play as much as possible in the second. Then play equally in both. Going into a friend's house, if the pup is reluctant to play, stop playing in your own house but tease the pup a little with the toys. Then play only in your friend's house. When you are successful, return to playing in both environments.

The same techniques are applied to each area you want to take the pup into. The reasons behind this are covered in detail under Socialisation, page 50.

Who should play with the pup?

I have to state here that the responsibility for play education must rest with the adult members of a family. The greatest bond between a young puppy and any other animal is that which develops through play.

That's why a few owners tell me that their dog doesn't play, when what they mean is it doesn't play with *them*, but they have another dog that it plays with! (See Chapter 6, Owning More than One Dog.) If the owners do not have the necessary time and patience to play educational games with a puppy then I suggest they should never have acquired that puppy in the first place. It would have been much wiser to have bought a tank of tropical fish.

Once the owners have started the play process, all the members of the family should play the basic games, possibly with one or two variations but under the same set of rules. Once the pup will play happily with all of the family then you can introduce other people who visit to the games – always under supervision of the owners. If the pup is a little shy of strangers or reluctant to play, use the technique previously mentioned under the heading Play environment on page 48. That means reducing the amount the owners play with the pup and introducing one or two known friends to encourage it to play in a familiar play environment. What we want the pup to learn is that people in general are wonderful things because they produce toys and play games, but ALWAYS UNDER THE SAME SET OF RULES. Remember, throughout the dog's entire life we want it to enjoy playing games. Controlling these games does not in any way mean that they should become dull or uninteresting. It is simply a matter of striking a balance between enthusiasm and control. When I produce a toy I expect any of my dogs to get excited immediately. The toy is more of a distraction than anything going on around it; play is enthusiastic and energetic and also demands a degree of mental agility. When I say 'that's enough', even though, with an adult dog, I am still holding the toy in an accessible position, I expect the dog to accept that is the end of the game. Control the games and you invariably control the dog. Let the dog control the games and the owner invariably ends up with little or no control over the dog.

Socialisation

This can be divided into three categories: a) the environment, b) people and children other than the owner's, and c) other dogs. At this point I should mention that the socialisation process I am referring to is a continuation of that which should have been started by the breeder and relates to puppies of up to sixteen weeks of age. If you acquired your dog at any age over sixteen weeks, then you should read Chapter 4, Re-homing a Dog.

After a few days the puppy should be used to all of the normal everyday sounds in the household in which it now lives. If for any reason it appears to be worried about any specific sounds, such as a vacuum cleaner or central-heating boiler switching on or off, simply arrange the next few meal-times and play sessions to coincide with the sounds that are causing the problem. The pup should very quickly learn that these particular noises always precede something extra pleasant happening and it should, therefore, lose any fear it might previously have had.

Next on the list comes the garden, into which the pup must never be allowed unaccompanied (see Housetraining, page 58), again using the play/feeding technique only if necessary to make expeditions into the garden a pleasurable experience.

ypical guard dogs. The territory is defined by either the length of the tether
ain or by the extent of the boundary fence

rsonal protection dog. These dogs always operate under the controlling
fluence of the handler who must be in attendance at all times (Guard Dogs
t 1975)

Below left: A bitch should remain calm and friendly when anyone handles the puppies in her presence. Any apprehension about humans on her part could easily be transmitted to the pups

Below right: Short coated breeds need to be groomed daily the same as long coated breeds. It is much easier to teach a small puppy to accept being touched and handled than it is to wait until it grows bigger and stronger. Note that a soft brush must be used initially

Above left: If your puppy has been taught to accept being groomed and handled then the process of touching it whilst it is eating is much less likely to result in aggression

Above right: This puppy had been placed in a plastic bag and dumped over a wall to 'dispose' of it

Below: These puppies arrived at a welfare society as part of the pre-Christmas throw out

You will then also be in a position to stop the development of any undesirable games, such as digging up plants.

Now for the car. The best and safest way for any dog to travel in a car is in a purpose-built cage behind the back seat. These are infinitely preferable to the old style of dog guard which was designed to restrict the dog to the area behind the rear seats but which most dogs took great delight in pulling down or wriggling through. But it is of little use placing a young puppy in a cage and then expecting it to enjoy trips in the car. It is better first to acclimatise the pup to the car before actually starting the engine and moving away. Begin by placing the pup's meal in the back of the car, then carry the pup out and gently place it in the back with its food. Carefully close the tailgate, without slamming it, and open one of the side doors; climb in and sit on the rear seat while the pup eats its meal. If it seems reluctant to eat, don't worry, simply remove the pup and its food after five minutes and give it no further food until its next meal-time is due, when you repeat the process. If all goes well, within a few sessions the pup should look upon being placed in the back of the car as a very pleasant experience, linked with its food.

You can then place food and pup in the car, start the engine and then sit on the back seat as before while the pup eats. Then, after a few sessions when the pup takes no notice of the running engine, you can get someone else to sit on the back seat to reassure the pup while you drive quickly round the block while it is eating its meal. If, at any time the car is moving, the pup starts to show signs of travel sickness (i.e. constant dribbling, sleepiness or generally turning 'green'), then stop using food immediately and switch to using toys to make the car as pleasant an association as possible.

It is also advisable to take the pup, along with a small bag of tasty titbits and a favourite toy, into one or two friends' houses in order to continue the pleasant association you have started in your own house.

You can also carry the pup out along a fairly busy road, again using some titbits, preferably before a meal is due, to accustom the pup to traffic. Follow this by trips to various places such as the local park, shopping centre, etc., maintaining the toys and food theme to get the pup to relax and enjoy the experience.

At this point I realise that a lot of people will say that it is wrong to take out a puppy under age of sixteen to eighteen weeks until it has completed a course of vaccinations, particularly because of the risk of parvovirus. The risk involved in isolating a young puppy from the environment in which it is required to live until it is over sixteen weeks is so great in terms of ending up with behaviour problems, that I personally would always take that risk. With new vaccines being developed that can be administered as early as six weeks of age, it would be as well to check with your vet before deciding on a socialisation programme. I firmly believe that the threat of parvovirus has resulted in more dogs being humanely destroyed because of behaviour problems that occurred due to little or no socialisation during the critical period than were ever killed by the disease itself. You must make up your own mind on this matter.

Socialisation with people

If you have had no trouble over the first few days getting the pup to enjoy your company and the company of the rest of the family, it seems logical that socialising it with other people should be simple and straightforward.

Some people's idea of socialisation consists of taking the young dog into a crowded shopping centre in the belief that this will get it to enjoy the company of other human beings. That is like saying that if you take the pup to a busy airport, it will get to enjoy the companionship of aeroplanes! Owners in fact frequently report that their adult dogs behave acceptably when walked among crowds but will not, without extreme difficulty, walk past a single figure standing at a bus stop. Taking a young puppy in among a crowd of people does little or nothing to socialise it with individuals; it simply gets it used to that environment.

The socialisation process can be started with people other than the owners by having one or two friends and neighbours come into the house, mix up the puppy's food and then feed it.

When taking the puppy out to meet people, always go out before a meal is due and take a few tasty titbits with you in a polythene bag. The rule is that the food is offered by whoever you happen to meet but the pup is not allowed actually to eat it until the person has touched the dog on the chest. The reason for touching on the chest is because the pup will feel more relaxed knowing that the person's hand remains in full view throughout. With a pup that is a little wary of being touched by a stranger, running a hand over its head and down its back will generally result in the pup spinning round in order to keep its eyes on the hand that is bothering it. Once the pup has been touched on the chest briefly then it is given the food. This touch gradually turns into stroking on the chest before the food is given. Because the puppy should start to learn very quickly that being stroked, in itself a pleasant experience, is accompanied by being offered and then given food, it should start attempting to make more and more voluntary contacts with people it meets.

By the time the puppy is twelve weeks old you can use games or a favourite toy, first of all in conjunction with, and ultimately as a replacement for, food in making good, positive social contacts with people in general. A word of caution perhaps would not go amiss here, and that is to remember not to over-stimulate a young puppy to the point where it becomes a nuisance and starts to pester everyone it meets for food. That is why using toys is, in the long term, a much better idea as you should have complete control over games and toys.

It is extremely important that the pup makes good, reward-ing social contact with all types of people it is likely to encounter during its expected life span of ten to fifteen years. Be sure to include adult males and females, trying to include anyone living locally of a different race from your own and also all of the tradespeople that call regularly such as postmen, dustmen, etc. Even if you do not have children, particularly young children, of your own, it is vital that the puppy learns that children are basically friendly and playful before it is sixteen weeks of age. Remember that most children will willingly come up and stroke a seven or eight-week-old puppy and offer it food. Far fewer would approach a seven-month-old puppy, and no one would allow a child near an eighteen-month-old dog that was growling menacingly because it was frightened about a child approaching.

So unless you are going to isolate your puppy from children for the whole of its life, you must introduce it to them and make

every effort to ensure that any introductions are as pleasant a
rewarding as possible.

The one category of person with whom it is difficult
socialise a dog is your vet. That's because the pup's first con
with the vet, for inoculations via an injection, is often
unpleasant experience. To overcome this it may help to b
the pup in for a general examination and health check after
get it home.

Arrange to take the puppy around the time a meal is due a
take that meal with you to the vet's in a plastic container. Al
the pup to eat its meal while it is being examined and if the p
seems relaxed and confident, ask the vet to inject it while
eating. If, on the other hand, it seems a little on edge, allow i
finish part of its meal and book the pup in for its injection
following day. You should find that when you return the sec
day the pup should be visibly more confident and rela
because the previous day's experience was enjoyable a
rewarding and nothing unpleasant happened.

If at any stage in your socialisation with people programme
hit any problems with one particular person, ask yourself why
pup should have taken a dislike to them. Was it the way t
approached the pup? Did something happen to frighten it.
their appearance any different from other people that the pup
met in the past, i.e. a man with a beard or wearing glasses
smoking a pipe, etc.? You should be able to isolate w
specifically is causing the problem and take steps to overcom
either by giving the person an external item of your clothin
wear during the next few encounters, effectively making t
person smell of you, or, where possible, by making yourself l
more like them by borrowing a pipe or a pair of glasses a
wearing them yourself for the next few play sessions. All of
must be completed by the time the pup is sixteen weeks of age i
all possible, to minimise any future problems.

Socialisation with other dogs

If the puppy that you now own is not the only dog in y
household, then it would be advisable first to read Chapte
Owning More than One Dog.

The problem about socialising a young pup with other d

is that other dogs will be far more exciting in terms of playing games than most owners would ever be, and once a young dog starts to become over-excited in playing games, the owner can often completely lose control of the games. This is particularly true in terms of games involving aggression with the use of teeth as the pup grows older. Remember, when you taught your puppy the rules of the games it played with you, one of them was that it must not put its teeth on any part of your body. This rule must surely also apply to other dogs that it meets and plays with (see Chapter 8, Dog/Dog Aggression), that is, the owner must remain in control throughout the game.

I would be extremely upset if any of my own dogs showed a preference for playing with other dogs in the area when exercised rather than wanting to play with me. But if you do little to play games or make yourself a really exciting person to be with, don't be surprised if your dog prefers the company of other dogs. Correct social contact should be carried out using only dogs known to have a good temperament with other dogs. Allowing a puppy to go running up to sniff at every dog you meet is definitely not the right way to go about it. If you take your pup towards an older dog that is aggressive – and by the way, don't think that an older dog would never bite or harm a puppy, lots do – and the puppy gets bitten, what good will that do to the pup's social contact with other dogs? That is similar to allowing a total stranger to come up to your pup and kick it, which in most cases will do untold damage to the pup's previously friendly disposition. So the rule is, if you do not know the other dog, no social contact is better than the wrong social contact.

Puppy socialisation and temperament training classes which are now starting to catch on in this country, due to the recent efforts of American vet, trainer and dog behaviourist Dr Ian Dunbar, are an excellent way of teaching your puppy correct social contact with other dogs under the experienced eye of a training instructor. The pups are taken along at between twelve and sixteen weeks of age and learn to play games that are acceptable and under the control of their owners, who take along toys and titbits in order to carry out the training. The classes also provide a degree of socialising with other people and children.

You must, however, ensure that the one you attend is run by a good, competent instructor who has had a great deal of experience in training puppies. Otherwise, if the class is chaotic with larger pups being allowed to intimidate smaller, shy pups, you could do far more harm than good. It would pay to sit in on the class for a couple of weeks to observe before actually enrolling for a course of lessons – which, incidentally, should not be expensive.

If you can't find a suitable puppy-training class then you will need to enlist the help and co-operation of other dog owners in your locality. Allow your pup to meet and play with any dog of whose temperament you are certain. If at any time the pup starts to become over-excited, or begins playfully to growl, bare its teeth or bite, stop the game immediately in the same way as when you taught control on a toy. Wait for the pup to calm down before either playing with a toy yourself or allowing the pup to play gently with the other dog again. Several times during play call the pup back to you, reward it with food or produce a toy after you have it under control, and invite a game. It is vital that, if a pup does not respond to your call, the owner of the other dog immediately controls it by making it sit or lie down, thereby making it much less inviting for the pup to continue playing with and making you, with the offer of food and a favourite toy, a much more attractive proposition. You can now continue in the same manner as you did when teaching control during games of chase by occasionally meeting the other dog and not allowing the pup to play, calling your pup back when it is running towards the other dog to play, etc. In other words you are re-teaching all of the lessons previously learned on toys, but now applied to other dogs. The idea is to keep you, the owner, in complete control of the game. This should not in any way reduce your dog's desire to play but you must remember not to become lazy and allow your pup to play more with other dogs than it plays with you and other members of your family.

Teaching the new puppy a few 'human' pack rules

The first rule is to teach the pup that it cannot expect to have contact with you for twenty-four hours a day, 365 days a year. If this is what the pup is allowed to believe then don't expect ever to be in a position to go out of the house and leave it alone, even for a few minutes, without the dog showing its objection in the form of barking, howling or chewing.

To start the process of teaching the pup to be by itself for short periods of time simply place its sleeping basket in the kitchen or hallway and, particularly after a play session when the pup shows signs of being tired and wanting to go to sleep, place it in its bed, go quickly and quietly out of the room and close the door. As the pup is tired, even if it does not settle straight away, ignore it and it should soon curl up in its bed and go to sleep.

Once it has been asleep for ten minutes or so, quietly open the door an inch or two and leave it that way so that when the pup wakes up it can get to you easily in order that you can take it out to relieve itself (see Housetraining, page 58). If you leave the door closed and the pup wakes up after fifteen minutes, it will start scratching at the door, yapping or howling to attract attention. If you go in when you hear this there is a chance that you will teach the pup that this sort of undesirable behaviour is rewarded by your attention and it will bark, howl and scratch the door with renewed vigour each and every time it is left. If, on the other hand, you choose the correct procedure of not entering the room until the puppy is quiet you will probably go in to find that the pup has been bursting to go to the toilet and has relieved itself on the floor, which doesn't exactly help the housetraining process. Leaving the door slightly ajar once you are certain that the pup is fast asleep gives you the best of both worlds: it will learn that if it barks or scratches at the door it never brings the owner back to 'reward' its undesirable behaviour but still gives it access to its owners when it needs to attract their attention to relieve itself.

If the above routine is carried out three or four times when the pup gets tired during the first day, it makes going to bed on the first night a lot easier for the pup to accept. Before you go to bed, spend some time playing with the pup and when you have finished the game, wait for the pup to show signs of becoming sleepy.

Place it in its bed in the chosen room and then produce your 'trump card'. Remember the piece of material you received from the breeder in a polythene bag (see page 34). If you open the bag, remove the bedding and place it in the pup's bed, along with a warm hot-water bottle, and then switch out the light the pup will do exactly what it did in the litter – it will smell the sleeping area and quickly curl up on the warm blanket and fall fast asleep in the comfort of the surrounding smell of mum and its brothers and sisters! The one thing that it can easily relate to in this new strange environment. Repeat the process every night for the first week.

As from day two, make sure that if you go from one room to the next for a few minutes, you remember to close the door behind you. If you allow a young puppy to follow you from room to room, it will become progressively more and more difficult to go out of the pup's sight and there is every chance that the young dog will then start to display signs of separation anxiety when it is away from the owner. An acquaintance of mine owned a dog which was nursed to sleep on his lap and was allowed to sleep curled up on his stomach on the settee at night for the first few weeks in his home. By the time that dog was a year old, it would tear down doors to get to him when he tried to leave it – even if he was sitting in the next room! During an enforced spell in kennels the dog became totally hysterical and had to be brought into the house, where it had the company of the kennel owners, for its own safety and well being.

It is very easy to condition a young puppy to accept being by itself for short periods providing there are plenty of games, attention and affection shown when you are present.

Housetraining

Puppies purchased from reputable breeders are almost always housetrained when they leave for their new homes and so housetraining is simply a continuation of the process started in the litter. During the daytime, when you are present, it is up to you to take the puppy out whenever it is most likely to want to relieve itself, i.e. when waking up, immediately after eating and after an energetic play session. It is simply a question of anticipating when the pup will want to go and then accompanying it to the chosen area in order to praise it when it performs where you want it to. The other 'danger sign' to watch for is rapid circling and trotting around, nose to the floor sniffing. If the almost inevitable accident occurs do not punish the pup but clean up and treat the soiled patch with biological washing powder diluted in water. Disinfectants will only put a second smell on top of the first smell which means that at any time in the next week or so if the pup smells the disinfected patch it will be very likely to relieve itself there again, believing that it is an acceptable toilet area. The disinfectant smell fools only human beings! You should also take note that all trips into the garden should be accompanied, particularly where house-training is concerned. If you put a puppy out into the garden by itself and then close the door it will then concentrate on trying to get back in. After ten minutes or so the owner then lets it back in believing it has relieved itself outside only to find that as soon as it comes back in, it relieves itself on the doormat! Even if the pup does in fact relieve itself outside the owner is never there to reward the pup for the correct behaviour – it only gets punished for the wrong behaviour.

It is too much to expect a young puppy to be clean overnight when left and so it is advisable to place a sheet of polythene down before you put several layers of newspaper on top. The top sheet should be dabbed with a spot of the pup's urine, and you should ensure that there is no danger of any dampness soaking through to the flooring beneath. If the floor itself gets damp, when you remove the newspaper in several weeks' time when the pup is old enough to last the night, it will still continue to soil where the newspapers were originally placed because of

Simple housetraining box comprising a wooden frame to contain papers, a polythene sheet and several layers of newspapers

the smell on the floor. The reason that you put a spot of the pup's urine on the top paper, by the way, is to help the pup find the toilet area that you have provided for it when it wakes up in the dark. It will quickly smell the area and relieve itself there and then happily return to bed. If the floor does get damp, remember to use biological washing powder to clean up. You must always make sure that the pup is taken out to relieve itself last thing at night before going to bed. It is also useful to remember that running exercise will generally stimulate bowel and bladder movement, while a slow walk around the garden will not be nearly as effective.

By the time the pup is six months of age it should be perfectly clean in the house. If it isn't, then first get it checked by your vet as there may be physical reasons for the problem, and after your dog has been given a clean bill of health, refer to the Section on Housetraining problems (page 162).

Introduction to collar and lead

The best time to introduce your puppy to the idea of wearing a collar is around a week after you get it, by which time it should be playing fairly enthusiastically when invited to do so. You can now slip on a soft puppy collar just before you start playing with a toy, leaving it on for the duration of the game. Don't worry unduly if the pup rubs its neck up against the furniture or tries to scratch it off, just persist in encouraging it to join in the game. You can also attach the collar a few minutes before feeding the pup, the idea being to make having the collar put on part of a pleasant, enjoyable experience. If you now gradually extend the time that the collar is in place, you should have the puppy completely accepting it by the time two weeks have elapsed. You can then progress to attaching a lead. Put on the collar and attach the lead whenever one of the pup's meals is due. Pick up the puppy, carry it into the next room and get someone to show the pup its food. Then ask them to place the bowl of food in its usual position and allow and encourage the pup to walk towards it, gently holding the lead in your hand. Under no circumstances should you drag it on the lead. You can progress in stages, each day moving further from the food bowl until the pup will quite happily walk the length of the house on the lead. The next stage is to carry the pup outside, a short distance away from the house, and let it walk back to its meal.

Once you can achieve this easily over a distance of a couple of hundred yards or so, the next stage is to get it to walk out and away from the house. This is where the process that you went through in getting the pup used to the car comes in handy. Park the car about fifty yards away from the house with the pup's meal in the back and, using as much encouragement as you can, walk the pup out of the house towards the car. When you reach the car, lift the pup into the back, let it eat its meal, then drive the fifty yards home. You can extend the distance gradually as long as you do not overtire your puppy by insisting that it walks too far. If you have got the pup used to being carried out and about to get it acclimatised to the sounds of traffic, etc. before the lead goes on, then walking on a collar and lead should present no problems at all. Most instances of adult dogs being frightened to go out of the house and refusing to walk on a lead have been caused by the owners putting on a collar and lead for the first time and trying to drag the pup out into the street when it has never had the experience of being in that environment. The whole process of having the collar on its neck, being pulled on the lead and frightened by the people and traffic proves far too traumatic for the pup who then understandably starts to suffer from agoraphobia!

Grooming and handling

If you took the advice given in Chapter 2, Selecting a Puppy, you should have started off with one that accepted the breeder handling and grooming it. Your responsibility is to continue and extend this process. This means at least one grooming session every single day for the first six months of its life and as often as necessary to keep the coat in good condition thereafter, which will obviously vary from breed to breed dependent on the coat type.

The groomer should gently insist that the pup stands reasonably still while it is groomed in the manner demonstrated by the breeder. If the pup starts to throw itself around to avoid being groomed, particularly behind the ears and between the hind legs, quickly restrain it, if necessary by enlisting the help of a second person, and continue when the pup has given up the struggle. If it tries to lie down, gently lift it back up again and continue each session until the pup totally accepts being groomed all over, at which point it can be praised, released and either allowed to play with a toy or given a meal. Within two weeks of acquiring a puppy it should totally accept being groomed by everyone in the family. Children should always groom the pup under adult supervision.

Once this has been achieved the next stage is to introduce a quick examination either immediately before or after the grooming session. Look into the pup's ears, open its mouth and check its teeth (remembering to do this gently when the pup is teething), lift up and examine each paw in turn, check in between the pads and the length of the nails and lift and check under its tail. While you are doing this, have a tasty titbit ready to give to the pup at any time during the examination as an extra reward for behaving the way you want.

It is also useful to get one or two friends to carry out this examination with a young puppy to accustom it to being handled by strangers. As this is one of the most valuable of all early lessons, never try to rush it or omit it altogether and remember that everyone in the family must take a turn in grooming, not just Mum or Dad. If at any stage during the grooming/handling process you start to run into serious difficulty, contact your vet who will put you in touch with either a professional groomer or a member of the Association of Pet Behaviour Consultants (APBC) who will show you the way to improve the pup's behaviour.

By the time the pup is six months of age it should accept and enjoy grooming and handling sessions, which now makes the pup so much easier to handle for owners, the general public, vets, trainers and judges alike.

Protecting food

You man be unfortunate enough to have purchased a puppy that has learnt to growl over its food when approached. This can become a major problem and should be stopped immediately. It often starts when the litter of puppies are fed out of a single bowl of food and the pups have to fight for their share. It is quite often the more submissive pups that learn to defend food, as their very survival depends on it. Where the breeder has the foresight to feed the puppies from individual bowls, food guarding develops only on extremely rare occasions.

The first rule is to ensure that the only time food is available in the pup's bowl is at meal-times, which should always be planned to follow the owner's meal-times. Dogs are pack animals and it is always the most important dogs in a pack that eat first. Feeding a dog before the family eats tells the dog that it is more important then the rest of the family with whom it lives, which tends to encourage it to become more dominant. Feeding it after the family have eaten tells it every day of its life that it is the least important member of the pack and therefore the most submissive, improving its respect for the owner's authority.

Place the bowl containing the food on the floor and allow the pup no more than ten minutes to eat it. Any food remaining after this time is to be removed and no further food offered until the next meal is due. Make a point of approaching the pup while it is eating and offer some really tasty treat such as cooked liver or chicken in exchange for its bowl. When it accepts the titbit, pick up the bowl, praise lavishly and put a little more chicken or liver on top of its meal before replacing it for the pup to eat. It should quickly learn that relinquishing its food bowl is rewarding rather than threatening and any growling should stop after a few repetitions. If your puppy shows signs of growling over food, be careful not to feed the pup lots of titbits from your hands as it can then easily start to growl whenever anyone comes near you, believing that you are some kind of food bowl. It is far easier to place any treats in the pup's bowl and allow it to eat them from there while you are correcting its undesirable behaviour. So, within a week of acquiring your pup it should be well mannered over food and you can then occasionally hold on to the food bowl while the puppy is eating and gently stroke it at the same time. Once the puppy accepts that you are not competing for the food, it should relax and accept anyone going near it while it is eating. If, despite carrying out the foregoing instructions, you still experience problems, then turn to Chapter 9, Other Behaviour Problems.

Destructive behaviour

All puppies chew to a certain extent, but it is important to
reduce chewing to a minimum to avoid the possibility of it
becoming a severe behaviour problem in later life, particularly
when the owner goes out and leaves the dog by itself.

The three principle causes of a young puppy chewing are
boredom, attention seeking and teething. You can perhaps now
see the importance of spending time playing with a puppy,
which should alleviate most cases of boredom. If the puppy is
provided with a large hide chew, marrowbone or 'Nylabone' at
such times when it is impossible to devote time to playing with
toys, this should engage the pup's mind and also help it through
the teething process. The chew or bone should be made
available only for short periods of time, for example if you have
to go out and leave the pup by itself for a little while. If it is left
available for the pup to chew on constantly it will quickly get
bored with that and progress to other things to chew that are
unacceptable to its owners. Casual, exploratory chewing of
items such as edges of carpet, chair legs or cushions can often be
prevented by spraying on a taste deterrent such as Bitter Apple.
This makes them taste unpleasant to the pup and is infinitely
preferable to the owner constantly nagging and punishing it. If
you see the pup chewing at anything that it is not supposed to
and you tell it off, followed by giving it a toy to amuse itself or a
bone to chew on, you will almost certainly end up with an adult
dog that chews anything and everything as soon as the owner
goes out, just to gain attention. This is detailed fully in Chapter
9, Other Behaviour Problems.

It is far wiser to administer 'environmental correction' rather
than make yourself look aggressive to the puppy. Environmental correction is where the pup is engaged in some activity
that the owner finds unacceptable and the pup receives a mildly
unpleasant shock which it associates with the action it was
carrying out. This 'shock' should in no way be associated with
the owner. A really useful device to keep handy is a set of 'dog
discs'. These are thin discs attached to a ring which can be
rattled and thrown to cause a minor distraction to the pup's
unwanted activity; they were invented by John Fisher, a

colleague of mine who is also a dog behaviour consultant, trainer and founder member of the Association of Pet Behaviour Consultants. The discs are extremely effective in preventing unwanted behaviour from developing but it must be remembered that the best plan, wherever possible, is to encourage and reward good behaviour rather than constantly correct bad behaviour.

Review of the first six months

If you take a good long look at your puppy when it is six months of age, it should have learnt a tremendous amount necessary for its survival within your human pack. The following checklist may be of benefit in deciding if there are any areas left that require a little more effort on your part. Your six-month-old puppy should:

1. Really enjoy playing games with your set of toys and you should have good control of all the games , being able to start and stop them almost at will.
2. Your pup should also be able to concentrate on play for longer periods and the games you provide should be both mentally and physically stimulating.
3. You should have a good measure of control when it plays with other people, particularly children.
4. The pup should accept all the human beings that it meets in a friendly manner without being too pushy.
5. It should show no apprehension when handled and examined and should look forward to its daily grooming session.
6. It should enjoy car travel without the slightest sign of fear or resentment.
7. It should enjoy the company of other dogs but should always remain under the controlling influence of the owner when playing.
8. It should enjoy short excursions on a collar and lead without showing any fear of the environment into which it is taken.
9. It should also have learnt correct social contact with other dogs without any signs of aggression or fear.

10.   It should have been allowed some contact with any other livestock that it may encounter on a regular basis but should not have been allowed to play with either farm animals or game.

11.   It should be perfectly happy to be left on its own for an hour or two while the owner goes out.

12.   It should accept whatever sleeping arrangements you make for it without showing resentment by crying, barking, etc.

13.   It should be perfectly clean in the house both during the day and when it is left at night.

14.   It should be totally non-aggressive over food and accept that, when food is on offer, it eats last.

15.   Almost all chewing should have stopped.

16.   It should understand a few simple control commands and should understand the cue or signal for a play session.

17.   It should never see its owners as bad-tempered and unpredictable.

18.   It should never see punishment as part of daily life with its owner.

19.   It should never be afraid of its owners but should respect and admire their higher status.

And above all else:

20.   It should still be allowed to be a puppy, so don't expect it to be perfect in every way at this age; it's just not fair on the pup. It will still get into mischief, it will still make mistakes, it still needs a kind, understanding owner who will take the time, trouble and patience to continue its education, but by this age you should have laid excellent foundations on which to build the ideal pet or working companion that you wanted when you first thought of owning a dog.

If you have successfully survived the first six months and have overcome all the pitfalls and problems involved in educating a young puppy, I can assure you that it gets much easier from now on. If you still retain the same enthusiasm for your pup as you did the day you took it home, then you are probably going to be an ideal companion for your dog.

4

Re-homing a Dog

The original idea of most charities involved in trying to re-home dogs was to provide a safe refuge for dogs that had inadvertently strayed away from their owners until they could be reclaimed, or to find new suitable homes for dogs which, through no fault of their own, had to leave the original household in which they were placed, because of bereavement, moving into an environment not suited to or not allowing the inclusion of a pet dog, marriage break up, etc. Most such 'shelter' kennels, however, quickly became convenient dumping grounds for fed-up owners who wanted a guilt-free way of disposing of a dog that had proved too troublesome to own, and unfortunately this continues to be the case to the present day.

A survey carried out in 1988 by one of the major animal welfare organisations into the reasons people part with their pets revealed that over one-third did so because of their dogs having behaviour problems, but were nevertheless quite happy about passing on these problems to other prospective owners. Despite the reasons given by the other two-thirds I would estimate a large proportion of these were parting with their dogs because they had behaviour problems but were not admitting it in case the dog was not accepted for re-homing. It has to be a very unusual set of circumstances that would make a family want to part with a perfectly well-behaved family pet that has grown up to be an excellent companion.

This is not to say, of course, that you cannot obtain a perfectly good family pet from a dog shelter, as some owners are incredibly intolerant about the slightest problem that arises with their pet and when the novelty of owning a pup wears off, will part with it at the least excuse. But the chances of taking home a dog free of any problems is fairly remote.

The reasons people want a dog from a shelter are usually twofold. Firstly they want to give a dog that may not have had the best start in life a second chance. The second, more common reason is that they want an older dog that is over the chewing stage and is already housetrained. These two reasons, however, are unfortunately the main reasons dogs are disposed of, along with aggression towards their previous owners and aggression towards children. So make absolutely certain the dog you get from a shelter or rescue is really the dog you want and does not have problems that you will not be able to cope with. If problems do in fact develop, it is incredibly difficult for behaviour consultants to advise on a course of corrective action because they have insufficient background to work with. If you can't identify the cause, it is difficult and sometimes impossible to advise on a cure.

Having said all that, it is a very satisfying and rewarding experience re-homing a dog that has perhaps been neglected or even ill-treated by the human beings with whom it had the misfortune to find itself living. The bond and trust that then builds up between the new owner and dog will last for its entire lifetime.

So if you want to re-home a dog, where do you go from here?

You must first decide what sort of dog you want in terms of size and approximate age. If you are looking for a particular breed then it is a good idea to find out where that breed rescue society is in your area. You should be able to get this information from the nearest animal welfare organisation or from the secretary of the breed club in question, whose name and address you can get from the Kennel Club if you enclose an SAE for reply. If you are not too particular about the breed, then make a phone call to your nearest shelter kennels (enquire at your local police station, vet's or training class) giving details of the type of dog you are interested in owning. Try to specify whether you want a dog or bitch, large, medium, small or toy, long- or short-coated and an approximate age and they should be in a position to tell you if they have anything that may be suitable. If they haven't then my advice is not to go along to the kennels to see what is available or I will guarantee that you will come away with the sort of dog you may not even have thought about owning prior to your visit. It is a heart-wrenching experience walking along rows of kennels with most of the dogs appearing to be begging for you to take them home.

When you finally locate a dog that meets your basic set of requirements, go along to the kennels but before you actually go to see the dog it would be well worth your while asking a few questions about its background. The following questions should provide you with a set of information on which to make a decision when you finally get to see the dog.

1. Ask about the environment the dog came from. How many people lived in the house? Were there children in the family? Did the family own another dog or any other pets?
2. Ask if the person who presented the dog for re-homing was its original and only owner or have there been more?
3. Ask the reasons given for parting with the dog.
4. Ask if the dog has previously been re-homed unsuccessfully by the shelter.
5. Ask how long the dog has been in the kennels.
6. Ask about its general behaviour with:
   a) kennel staff
   b) other dogs
   c) other visitors.

If you are concerned about the answers you receive to any of the above questions, then say so. The staff are there to help you make the right choice and it is in their own, and the dog in question's interest to ensure that both the dog and you are right for one another. They certainly would not want you to take away a dog that they know will be returned as unsuitable a week or so later.

You should now be prepared to answer a whole host of questions that you will be asked in order to decide if you are able to provide a suitable home for the dog. It is vital that you answer each question honestly and accurately so that the dog's future well being is assured.

If you are happy about the answers you receive and the kennel management has no objections to you being the prospective new owner, then go and have a look at the dog in its kennel, if possible taking the whole family along.

When you approach the kennel, how does the dog behave? Does it retreat to a corner of the kennel and make low growling noises? Or does it race up to the kennel door barking furiously, and is its reaction the same with every member of the family? The way the dog behaves when you approach its kennel could well be the way that it will behave in your house when visitors arrive, once it has been allowed to settle in for a few weeks.

Now ask for the dog to be brought out of its kennel on a lead. How easy was it to get the dog on a lead? Once outside the territory of its kennel, its behaviour should immediately improve and if it seemed a little apprehensive to begin with, this should now disappear. If its behaviour deteriorates to the point of any display of aggression, then you should reject it as unsuitable.

The last thing that you need to observe is its general behaviour with other dogs as it passes along the kennels. If it flies at the kennels, barking furiously, then you will have to think carefully about taking it home, particularly if there are a number of dog owners in your locality. It is also a good idea to ask one of the kennel staff to groom it in front of you. The majority of staff employed at rescue or shelter kennels are experienced in handling dogs and so if they cannot manage to groom a dog that has already become familiar with them, you are unlikely to be able to either.

So now it's decision time, but rather than make a decision immediately, why not first take the dog out for a walk for an hour and discuss it among the whole family. If you make the decision to take the dog home, the welfare organisation will usually carefully outline the conditions under which you will be allowed to take up ownership. Remember that if the answers you received to any of your questions leave you in any doubt about your ability, expertise or patience to cope with and with luck modify the dog's behaviour then it is wiser to wait and make another choice when something more suitable comes along.

Once you have made a choice and arrive home with your dog, it is important to remember that it will take time to get to know it and similarly it will take time to settle into its new environment. The way you approach the first days your dog spends with you will depend, to a large extent, on its temperament. Every dog is an individual and a boisterous, headstrong dog that has had little in the way of formal discipline may need firmer handling than, say, a dog that is on the shy side which needs gentle handling in order to overcome its apprehension in its new surroundings. The important thing to remember is that it would normally take about fourteen days for the dog to establish itself in a new home and so it would be extremely unlikely to exhibit any particularly bad behaviour when you first arrive home with it. So in addition to trying to make the dog feel loved and wanted you must also monitor its behaviour closely in order to prevent any undesirable behaviour from developing and to watch for any danger signals. As it normally takes about two weeks for a dog to settle into a new environment, you can never be sure about the dog's behaviour until this amount of time has elapsed.

Before allowing your dog into the house, it would be wise to allow it to relieve itself by walking it around the garden. If it has come straight out of a kennel then into your car and out of the car and into your house, where it may at first feel insecure, not knowing where its permitted toilet area is, it will be likely to relieve itself on the living room carpet.

The following has to be the type of pattern that exists for the first fourteen days. The aim is to educate the dog into the rules and regulations under which you are providing the warmth, comfort, security and affection in the household. It is always preferable to anticipate a problem arising and take the necessary avoiding action rather than allowing a situation to develop where the dog is punished after he has broken a rule that he was ignorant about. It is better to assume that the previous owner taught the dog nothing at all and start afresh than to credit it with a basic understanding of the human values of right and wrong.

Your dog has a capacity to remember events that happened in its life before you acquired it, with events that were either very pleasant or very unpleasant being retained for the greatest length of time, sometimes for life. So be alert for any sudden changes in your dog's behaviour which may be triggered off by a particular sight, sound or smell. Some owners, for instance, chastise puppies by hitting them with a rolled-up newspaper. With a fairly sensitive pup this can be a really frightening experience with the result that if the dog is subsequently re-homed, if anyone picks up a newspaper it triggers off the same fear response even though the new owners have never chastised the dog at all. On the other hand, putting on your coat and picking up a lead should lead to a great deal of excitement on the dog's part, triggering off an earlier response to going out for a walk to the local exercise area.

Because you will not be aware of any pleasant or unpleasant associations your dog may have, it is always a good idea to change its name and give it a new identity, particularly if it is a young dog. This way you can be sure of introducing a pleasant association with the name of your choice.

Try to pick a short name that suits the character of the dog and try to avoid anything that sounds like its former name. Think of a dog whose previous owner has called its name to try to get it to return when exercising off the lead and then, when the dog was slow to respond, chased after it and smacked it. You can imagine that dog's response to a new owner calling its old name: at best it will appear frightened and reluctant to return; at worst it may run away, fearing the same treatment as it received from its former owner after hearing its name called.

It is also important, until you get the correct response when you call out the dog's new name, that you do not allow it to exercise off the lead.

After two weeks, when you are satisfied that the dog returns to you every time in the house or garden when called, you can try giving it some freedom in a larger area. The best place is an area that is completely enclosed by a fence so that if you do experience difficulty in getting your dog back, at least it cannot escape and possibly cause an accident. To make things easier for you attach a ten-foot length of cord to its collar before you detach the lead and let it run free, trailing the line behind it. The dog will be less likely to take off as it will feel the slight resistance of the line dragging on the ground and it will also avoid the necessity of you having to grab its collar in order to get it back on the lead. To regain control, simply put your foot on the end of the line to prevent the dog avoiding you, pick up the line and gently coax the dog towards you, using a titbit to reward him for returning. Once that you are confident that your dog will return every time it is called, you can dispense with the line.

One of the commonest mistakes is for the new owner to

overdo the fuss and attention their dog receives over the first week or so, after it has perhaps been in isolation in kennels for some considerable time. Occasionally the new owner will even take time off work to be with the dog twenty-four hours a day. Then the owner returns to work and the dog, deprived of all the attention it has become used to getting, suddenly finds itself alone and behaves in the only way it can to draw attention to itself – by barking, chewing or soiling. It is cruel to lavish uninterrupted attention on a dog for the first two days and then put it in a position where it is asked to cope with isolation. So the rule is to start from day one the way you want the dog to accept life as a member of your family. Start by teaching the dog to be by itself in the kitchen or another room for an hour or so while you sit in the adjoining room. It is best to wait until it is tired and is looking for somewhere to curl up and go to sleep of its own free will. Lead it to its bed, basket or blanket that you have provided in a quiet corner of the room, go into the next room and close the door behind you. Getting the dog used to spending several short periods of ten to twenty minutes by itself right from the start will prevent problems of separation anxiety later when the dog has to be left for slightly longer periods.

Housetraining must take place over the first few days and it is wise to assume that the dog is not housetrained to avoid unnecessarily punishing a dog for something he may not have been taught by his previous owners as unacceptable behaviour. It is up to you to find out the extent of what he does not know and then teach him what he should know.

Try to anticipate when he will want to relieve himself, take him out to your chosen spot in the garden and encourage him to 'perform'. Praise him well when he does so. If he does make an odd mistake then by all means tell him off verbally if you catch him in the act, then take him outside and praise him when he relieves himself where you want. If you happen to spot a wet or soiled patch on the floor after the dog has finished then it is of no use to offer any form of punishment as it would be unlikely to be associated with the crime of relieving himself – besides which you do not want to appear to be aggressive to your new dog. It may have learnt to deal with aggressive humans, thanks to its previous owners.

Although your dog may not want to play any games with toys

for the first few days, it will help him to relax and settle in if you can encourage some short sessions of gentle play as they will give you a really good idea of its likely temperament. It is possible that your dog will be very difficult to motivate to play games. That is often because the early part of its life has been spent in the company of another dog rather than with people. This is most often found when acquiring a puppy from a breeder when it is over sixteen weeks old, when it has spent most of its time with litter-mates or with its mum.

What is the dog's response to the production of a toy? If it becomes over-excited to the point of being difficult to control, you will have to be very careful to ensure that you educate it as to what constitutes acceptable and unacceptable play, as a dog that gets over-excited in play is likely to show the same sort of uncontrollable enthusiasm when visitors arrive, etc. Try throwing a toy and watch for the dog's reaction. Can you get the toy back off the dog easily or is it a battle of wits for you to recover it? If it is, it may mean that the dog has been possessive about toys and other items in its previous household. If on the other hand the dog attempts to tear the toy to pieces, then suspect that the dog has been allowed access to toys, old slippers, etc. to chew and may well have learnt to chew things that you would find unacceptable. If the dog brings the toy back and drops it in your hand, in your lap or on the floor in front of you then this would indicate that someone has devoted some time and patience in applying some formal education and rules to the games they have played with it.

Try to avoid games that involve the dog using you as a toy and make sure that, at the end of a play session, the toys are put away to where the dog has no access to them. This is particularly important if your dog enjoys playing games of tug-of-war, when you should insist that the dog gives up the toy when told to do so. This will give the dog the impression that you are both physically and mentally stronger than he is and will reduce the possibility of dominance problems later. Discourage games that involve the dog being teased or becoming over-excited and try to stop the game before it becomes bored.

It is also important that you carry out daily grooming/ handling lessons. As mentioned in the previous chapter, grooming must take place regardless of the length of the dog's coat.

With a re-homed dog it is, of course, possible that he is not used to being restrained and handled and he may well object by fidgeting, trying to escape or, worse still, becoming aggressive. To ensure that early grooming/handling lessons are acceptable and pleasant to the dog, go about it in the following manner. First of all attach its lead and collar then, if it is a smaller breed of dog, gently lift it up on to a table and fasten its lead to any convenient point. This now leaves both of your hands free and puts the dog in a position where it is easy to control. Have a small quantity of tasty titbits such as chicken or liver available nearby and pick up the grooming brush in one hand and a titbit in the other. Hold the hand with the titbit in just in front of the dog's nose with the food held between your fingers so that he cannot get at it. Very gently run the brush down his back from his shoulders to his tail, then open up your fingers and allow him to eat the food. Repeat several times more, praising and reassuring him as necessary.

At the next session either later the same day or the following

A dog fastened in preparation for a grooming session. This leaves both of the groomer's hands free to control the dog

day, repeat the process but start brushing at the top of the dog's head, just behind its ears, down to the tail as before. You can then progress each day until you are able to brush every part of the dog's body while it eagerly awaits the food rewards in your hand. You can then start examining the dog, just as a vet would do, by exchanging food for a look at all four paws, ears, teeth and last of all eyes. The purpose behind this is to ensure that any previous bad associations the dog has had with being touched, possibly with painful consequences, are slowly and gently turned into pleasant experiences. It is important that, once the adults have the correct response from the dog, the children are taught how to do the same under supervision.

Don't omit to do the above with your new re-homed dog as it may have had an injury in the past which makes it apprehensive about having the part in question touched and examined, and it is far better to find this out when you are in a position to control the dog and reward it when it relaxes and allows you to touch any particularly sensitive areas.

Introducing your re-homed dog to any other pets you may have has to be done carefully and when doing so you must take into consideration the fact that your dog may never have met other animals before and the whole experience may prove either exciting or frightening.

Initial introductions to household pets such as cats, caged birds, etc. should be carried out by placing the dog on a lead and ensuring that the other pet is able to move away to a safe place if it wants to. Wait until the initial excitement has died down before carefully allowing the dog to approach. You should try to remain casual and off-hand throughout, to reduce any over-excitement or anxiety on the dog's part. A few introductory sessions over the first few days should give you enough confidence to allow your dog supervised access to your other pets, either off the lead or, if you still have any doubts, with the lead attached but trailing on the floor just in case. Never make the initial introduction by showing your dog the other animal held in your hands. This will almost certainly lead to trouble as the other animal will feel trapped and will probably wriggle and try to escape as the dog approaches and this will increase the dog's excitement, or it may believe that you are teasing it with a toy of some sort. If, after two weeks or so, you are still having problems with your dog becoming over-excited with the other animal to the point of it being something of an obsession, then you will have to treat it as a behaviour problem, which is discussed fully in Chapter 9, Other Behavioural Problems.

Introducing your re-homed dog to another dog living in the same household also has to be carried out carefully if you want to avoid the possibility of aggression problems. Remember that the dog already living in your house will probably have some toys of its own, a bed or sleeping area, a feeding area and some favourite areas in which it relaxes. Bringing a strange dog into the house could easily be seen as a threat to the existing dog, particularly if the new dog comes in and immediately tries to take over or even approach one of the areas of privilege that the original dog has always enjoyed. It is far better to make the initial introduction on territory that is neutral to both dogs, and where neither dog has any possessions to defend. It is also a good idea, if you can manage it, to hold on to the new dog yourself and get someone else to hold on to your original dog – that way you remove the possibility of your existing dog defending you. Let both dogs approach and sniff one another, held on slack leads. Try not to interfere unless absolutely necessary and avoid trying to stroke either dog until they both start to relax. Remember that dogs have their own body language and methods of communication and trying to talk to and reassure both dogs will do little to speed up the process and may in fact serve only to increase the tension. After an hour or so of relaxed exercise you can walk both dogs home. It is better to avoid a car journey home unless it is absolutely essential because of possible problems related to territory and the fact that confining two dogs that have just met in a small area, without the means to escape if either feels threatened, will prevent both dogs from relaxing.

On arriving home, allow both dogs to enter and immediately remove your first dog's lead but leave your re-homed dog's lead attached and trailing. This will give you very quick control, in the unlikely event of there being any unpleasantness between them. You should have removed any toys, dog beds and food bowls prior to allowing the dogs into the house and it is important, for the first few days, that toys, chew bones, food bowls and bedding are provided only under close supervision until both dogs accept one another fully and cease to see one another as a threat.

Introducing your re-homed dog to children must be carried out very carefully and it is vital that your dog and children are not allowed any unsupervised access to one another whatsoever. First of all you should have established that the dog's behaviour was acceptable with children from the information given to you by the welfare organisation from which you obtained your dog. You should also bear in mind that the original owner may not have been totally honest in giving the correct information when they presented the dog for rehoming. For at least the first two weeks you must ensure that the dog does not feel crowded by the presence of a child or children who are perhaps desperate to shower him with affection. The dog must never feel trapped or hemmed in and parents should always see that the dog is provided with an escape route into another room if it wants to be by itself for a short while. Never allow a child to go over and stroke the dog during this settling-in period, but always make sure that the dog is called over to the child to be fussed and stroked. This then ensures that the dog has a choice and will feel confident to approach in the knowledge that it is not being forced into situations where it becomes worried. You should also bear in mind the fact that your dog may have been allowed to jump at children or play rough games with them and your child may well find such games frightening. You should ensure that the teaching process is a two-way affair. Teach the child how to approach and handle the dog; teach the dog how to approach and interact with the child. It is easier and kinder to establish ground rules from day one, rather than allow the dog to misbehave on the first few days only to chastise him a week later for the same behaviour. It is also important that your attitude towards the dog does not leave the children feeling deprived of attention and resentful of this new arrival into the family home. For further information, see Chapter 5, Children and Dogs.

Giving an unwanted dog a new home can be a tremendously rewarding experience and problems can be kept to a minimum by understanding that the dog will be both unsettled and confused at first and in need of a great deal of sympathetic handling. Once you have established the ground rules, which may differ greatly from those he is used to, and settled him into a routine, you can then begin the more formal training that will make him a pleasurable, loyal and affectionate companion for many years to come. Most of the people who manage successfully to re-home a dog get a tremendous amount of satisfaction from giving an unwanted dog a new start in life. The dog, for its part, often has an exceptionally strong bond with its new owner which is built upon mutual trust and understanding.

5

Children and Dogs

Each year millions of pet dogs find their way into animal sanctuaries, shelters and welfare centres for re-homing. Sadly very few are adopted or reunited with their owners, which means that the rest are put to sleep. The need to teach children about the responsibilities of owning a pet dog have never been greater than at the present time. When a dog is brought into a home where there are children, the whole family have taken on a commitment to look after, protect and educate the animal and it is in the education of our children that we must take the responsibility to teach a better understanding of our companion animals in order to stamp out neglect, abuse and exploitation. The careless disregard for animals by an alarming number of irresponsible people is bringing about a situation where the pet dog is becoming a commodity that may be easily disposed of in the manner that we use to dispose of an unwanted car. There is little doubt that children tend to learn a lot about their attitudes to other animals from their parents and so if we want a future generation that will improve the life and image of the pet dog in society, then we must all make an undertaking to embark on a programme of pet education both in our homes and in our schools.

Children, like our dogs, go through various stages as they grow up and this should be taken into account when a new puppy or older dog arrives in the home. It would be unwise to allow a five-year-old child to pick up a young puppy whereas, with care, a ten-year-old should manage with little difficulty provided he or she has been shown how. As a guide, I will attempt to outline what you should expect of both your child and your dog, taking into account the age of the child.

Maybe you already own a dog and you are worried about the imminent arrival of a new baby and how your dog will accept it.

Most dogs that exhibit the human emotion of jealousy when a new baby arrives do so because the whole of their lifestyle has been suddenly and dramatically changed. The attention that the dog used to receive is reduced and it finds itself pushed to the fringe of the pack. It also finds that there are now a few 'no-go' areas, such as the settee. Perhaps it used to be allowed to jump up when the owner returned home but now it is shouted at when the owner comes in carrying the baby and it attempts to greet them in the manner it has been used to. Some dogs that have been used to the privilege of sleeping in the owner's bedroom, possibly on the bed, find themselves relegated to the kitchen at night after the arrival of this new baby. The common problem of destruction or a sudden lapse in housetraining is created by the owners, who will increase their contact and affection for the dog for some weeks before the baby arrives as a form of compensation for the lack of attention it will receive after the birth. It is far better to get the dog into the routine that it will have to fit into three months before the baby arrives than to wait until the day of arrival when the dog will be in very little doubt as to what has caused this sudden change in its environment and lifestyle.

If you have never experienced any type of behaviour or control problems with your dog then there is no reason to assume that you will experience any problems due to a new baby coming into the 'pack'. Behaviour problems, particularly those related to dominance, will require very special handling techniques in order to ensure that the dog completely accepts the newcomer. This is beyond the scope of this book and will require the services of a vet or a dog behaviour consultant working with the individual dog and family. The problem of dominance is dealt with fully in Chapter 7, Dog/Human Aggression Problems.

The best way of introducing your dog to your new baby is to take the dog out for a walk and bring the baby into the house in its absence. Keep the dog out for an hour or so and give it lots of energetic exercise so that it is quite tired by the time you return home. Position the baby in an area with which the dog has little in the way of associations. The wrong places would be the settee, if the dog is usually allowed to jump on it; the rug by the fire, if the dog normally lies there to rest; the kitchen, where the dog is normally fed, or any other area where the dog may resent the sudden and unexpected intrusion. The ideal place to put the pram or cot would be a part of the living room where the dog would not normally spend much time, or a downstairs room that the dog rarely goes into. As soon as the dog enters the house he will notice the changes in the background smell and will want to investigate. You should allow him to go up and sniff at the baby, keeping him on the lead until the dog's investigation is complete, when he will turn away and probably appear uninterested. If you then give the dog a small feed to take his mind off the baby you will find that he will then return to have a further sniff and then settle down to rest or relax in his favourite spot. If you then go about your daily duties as if nothing has changed you should find that apart from the dog looking puzzled when the baby cries or moves, he accepts it without any problems. For the next few days, if you try to link one or two pleasant associations with the baby, like going out for a walk with the pram or a game with a favourite toy when the baby has been put to bed, you should find that your dog soon grows to enjoy the new arrival. Avoid trying to speed up the process by carrying the baby towards the dog to introduce it or by insisting that the dog goes over to say hello. When the baby is being held or cuddled, give the dog a chew bone or toy to play with as a special treat to help prevent it feeling unwanted and trying to push in for attention. It also goes without saying that even if your dog is of impeccable temperament, it should never be left with the baby without adult supervision even for a moment. The vast majority of pet dogs soon accept and enjoy the company of an addition to the family, but there are dogs that will not tolerate a small baby and in this instance it is wiser, and kinder on the dog, to consider re-homing it into an environment where there are no small children – although it must be said that the chances of your dog not tolerating your baby must be many thousands to one against.

Seven months to eighteen months

The most difficult stage for both dog and baby is the period when the baby is between seven and eight months of age. This

ove: The result of an owner not realising that a German Shepherd grows
ge and needs feeding! When the dog arrived at the Blue Cross Kennels she
s in poor condition having never been fed proper dog food

ow left: This puppy has now been successfully rehomed after being found
d up and abandoned in a grave yard

ow right: Appealing dogs begging to be rehomed or potential disasters?
member that a lot of dogs end up in rescue kennels because of behaviour
blems. You can rarely tell just by looking

Above left: Few children can resist the appeal of a young puppy, but remember that in eighteen months time these young puppies will be adult dogs, but the children will still be children

Above right: Strengthening the bond through education of both child and puppy

Below: Littermates like Jim, Frank, Toyah and Miss Houdini (guess which one is Miss Houdini) who have lived together all of their young lives, find it difficult to adjust to normal home environments when parted from one another

...ve: Understanding the ...ponsibilities of owning a ... should start at an early ... Classes such as this are ...nkfully becoming more ...mmonplace

...ht: The size of the dog ... choose will be an ...portant factor in deciding ... much control you ...w to a young child

Responsibility for the family dog's welfare can be increased with maturity, by which time a bond will have developed between both parties

Problems are easier to solve when there is only one dog involved, even if it is a simple pulling on the lead problem

is when the baby begins to crawl and is also when it will be more and more interested in exploring the world around it. It is also the time when the baby is becoming mobile enough to be introduced to the concept of playing with toys that are capable of sound and movement which the child itself can instigate and control in the environment previously reserved for the dog – on the floor. This means that any toys the dog previously enjoyed playing with are now accessible to the child's enquiring mind and at a stage where neither party will have little or no concept of sharing. This is why I have always advocated that the owners should control the dog's access to toys and why the dog should learn that he owns no toys right from the outset. It is then a simple matter to teach the dog that the child's toys can be played with only by invitation of the supervising adult. Because of the obvious difficulty in teaching such a young child the correct way to approach a dog, it is far better to provide the dog with a safe refuge in an area where the child cannot follow. This can be simply achieved by placing a piece of plywood across a doorway, held in place by hooks screwed into the door frame, over which the dog may jump without the child being able to follow (see illustration). This will prevent any

An escape route for the dog, through which the child is unable to follow

situations arising where the child continually crawls after the dog and will not allow it to settle down and relax. Some dogs start to get frightened when continually harassed by an unintentionally persistent child and may be pushed into snapping if they feel trapped and unable to escape. So it is far easier at this stage to teach the dog to move out of the child's way if it starts to become uneasy rather than to teach the child not to torment the dog.

When the child starts walking there is even more danger to the dog, particularly if it is lying on the floor asleep. It only takes a child who is unsteady on its feet to trip over the dog and startle it to produce an instinctive snap before the dog is aware of what it has done. It is also, of course, dangerous from the point of view of the child falling and injuring either itself or the dog. I am well aware that a great number of dogs are incredibly tolerant of unintentional abuse and are sat on and have their ears and tails pulled daily by very young children, but if everyone took steps to ensure that all early contact with dogs is supervised and that the dog learns that the alternative to tolerating this sort of abuse is to walk away, then we would have fewer problems with our dogs and our children.

By the time a child has reached the age of eighteen months it should be steady on its feet and less likely to trip over a resting dog accidentally. The child should also have been taught a sense of right and wrong or at least should know when you are pleased and when you are not. It is now a fairly simple matter to start including the child in the daily responsibilities of dog ownership. You can begin by teaching the child how to prepare the dog's daily meals, and provided you have no problems with your dog regarding food protection you can allow the child to tell the dog to sit before placing the food down for the dog. This simple act will start to introduce your child to the concept of reward training which is so important in continuing to build the bond between them as they both grow. Simple grooming sessions can then follow, again with the emphasis on rewarding the dog's correct behaviour. Hold on to the dog yourself while you teach your child to brush gently down the dog's back and down its sides. If you are clever you can use food preparation and grooming as a reward for your child's good behaviour, as most young children will take great delight in being allowed the privilege of interactions with the dog that have previously been reserved exclusively for the adult members of the family.

This is also the best age to teach the child not to abuse or ill-treat the dog. Consider the dog as if it were another, young child. Would you want your child to grow up thinking that it is acceptable to stand on it, kick it, poke its eyes or pull its hair? We are so often guilty of operating a double standard in our approach to other animals and are often taught by our parents to be thoughtful, kind and considerate to other human beings while being allowed to mistreat the family pet.

By using the same form of teaching with your child as you should with your dog, the whole process is relatively simple and straightforward. Each and every time your child interacts with your dog in a way that you find acceptable, i.e. stroking, sharing a toy, offering food, or any other act of kindness or consideration, then seize the opportunity to reward the child immediately by giving it some attention in the form of praise, followed if possible by an activity that the child enjoys. If, on the other hand, you see your child mistreating the dog, even in play, then try to explain carefully *why* their action was undesirable. It is not sufficient simply to say that they must not do it again, and it is unfair to punish the child for breaking a rule they were not aware existed in the first place. If the undesirable action is repeated, then the child must learn that the consequences of knowingly breaking the rules are un-rewarding. This can best be achieved by withholding one of the privileges relating to the dog or, if necessary, by calling a 'time out' by isolating the child in another room for a short period of time to contemplate the consequences of its former actions. You must exercise extreme caution to ensure that the child is not allowed to believe that you have more affection for the dog than for the child, and it is also essential that, because of the attention the child inevitably receives for abusing the dog, it is not encouraged to use abuse as a way of gaining attention. That is why it is important that if you use the 'time out' system the dog is not put out of the room but the child is. The success of the system depends on your ability to reward the child's good behaviour rather than correcting the child's bad behaviour. Parents are often guilty of telling their children all the things that they must *not* do without ever considering using rewards when the child behaves correctly, and good behaviour often goes unnoticed.

By the time the child has reached school age he or she should have complete trust and understanding of the family pet and this should be reflected in the dog's attitude towards the child. Between the ages of five and ten a child learns a tremendous amount about the world and when it is approached by another dog, the initial contact will be entirely dependent on the child's experience with your own dog. Although it may be permissible to approach your own dog, other dogs are a different matter and it is as well to teach your child the correct approach. First of all, not all dogs are as friendly as the one at home. Some dogs are frightened of children and may bite or snap if approached. Others, on the other hand, may have been teased and therefore be resentful and unapproachable. For this reason, it is essential that a young child is taught never to approach a dog that is not accompanied by its owner. It is also a good idea to teach the child always to ask the attendant owner before approaching the dog to stroke it. If, when the child is invited to stroke the dog, it starts to back away as the child approaches, then it is better not to stroke it at all, particularly if it is held on the lead. If the dog feels restrained and unable to get away it is far more likely to snap at an approaching child than it would have been if it were free to move away.

It is better if the child strokes the dog's chest and the top of its head, avoiding its back and hindquarters. A great many dogs will allow you to touch them provided that they can see your hands but when they lose sight of the hand that is touching them they are much more likely to spin round and possibly snap. It is also important that the child remains standing throughout, and maintains a height advantage over the dog. Children should also be taught never to put their faces close to a strange dog or try to cuddle it. A great many dogs will see that as a direct threat with disastrous consequences.

When your young child starts to bring home friends, particularly those who may be frightened of dogs, it is important that the visiting child is taught how to relate to the dog. Once again the rule must be that there is no unsupervised contact, so that the children and dog can benefit from one another's company. If the children are engaged in any rough or particularly noisy games it is better to put the dog in another room to avoid him becoming over-excited by the enthusiasm with which the children are playing. Wrestling games played by two or more children must definitely *not* be played when the dog is present as it may easily believe that your child is being threatened and take the necessary steps to protect him or her. To continue the theme of correctly socialising your dog with other children, when your child's friends call round it is an excellent opportunity to involve them in preparing the dog's meal or accompanying the family on a short walk with the dog, thus turning the arrival of another child into an enjoyable experience for the dog. If your child has also learnt to get the dog to respond to one or two simple control commands, then it is a good idea to allow a demonstration of how to get the dog to sit, come, stay, etc.

Remember that if you have always allowed your dog to jump up at you, if it jumps up at another child, who may not be used to dogs, it can be a terrifying experience even though the dog is only being friendly, and then, once the dog starts to realise that the child is frightened, it may well begin to bully them. Providing that you are sensible there is no reason at all why your dog should not accept and enjoy the company of any other child that your son or daughter brings home to play with.

Taking your child to and from school is another opportunity to socialise the dog with children and it also gives the child an awareness that your dog is a part of the family and a sense of pride in being connected to the dog their friends are admiring.

A well-mannered dog which is taken to school on a daily basis will also be particularly beneficial to all those children who have little or no contact with dogs in the early part of their lives.

Five to ten years of age

This is the age when most children who have never owned a dog start to pester their parents for one, using the argument that all their friends have one. Common sense must prevail as a child under the age of ten would be almost totally incapable of looking after the needs of a young dog and, without proper supervision, would certainly not have the time, patience or experience necessary to train it. When a puppy is purchased solely to satisfy a child's desires, it usually ends up unwanted when the initial novelty wears off, at best leaving Mum to look after it or, at worst, being re-homed or euthanased. What you have to ask yourself is: Who will feed it four times a day at first? Who will take it for exercise? Who will be responsible for socialising it? Who will housetrain it? Who will groom it and who will train it? If you decide that an adult wants to take on that responsibility assisted by your child, then by all means go out and purchase a puppy or take in an older dog from rescue; your child will gain a tremendous amount from learning to be a good, responsible dog owner under your guidance.

Between the ages of five and ten you can allow your child an increasing amount of responsibility for the dog's well being. Why not enrol at a ringcraft or dog-training club to involve your child in the dog's more formal education? Even if you have an older dog your child can only benefit from the experience as it is, despite popular opinion to the contrary, quite possible to teach an old dog new tricks. An increasing number of clubs cater for young children and there are even competition classes for junior handlers. Allowing your child to exercise more control over your dog, particularly on family outings, will make him feel more mature and important and will help to cement the relationship between them both.

You should also never underestimate the importance of your dog as an educational aid. The dog can be given as an example to illustrate diet, health and well being, exercise, and the world of nature. The question of human reproduction and of bereavement is also much easier for you to explain and for the child to understand if your dog is used to approach the subject.

Ten years onwards

Providing that you have never experienced any behaviour problems with your dog relating to the child, then it would normally be perfectly safe to allow them increasing amounts of unsupervised time together without the worry that either one will come to any harm. It is not advisable to leave a dog that you have taken in for re-homing within the last six months any free access to a child until you are absolutely certain of its temperament. You should also be in a position to allow short excursions when the dog may accompany your child to a friend's house, or out on a walk with friends. It would also be acceptable to allow your child the major responsibility in the dog's formal education under the guidance of a training instructor. It is also possible for a child of ten years of age or over to compete successfully against adults in any of the sports associated with dogs, such as Obedience, Working Trials or Agility.

Some of the more enlightened people in the field of education and animal welfare are now starting to introduce the concept of pet education into the school curriculum. 'As the twig is bent so grows the tree' is one of the mottos of the People Pet Partnership Programme run by the College of Veterinary Medicine at Washington State University.

The children of today are the dog owners of tomorrow and the future of the pet dog as we know it is in their hands, and it is up to each and every one of us to ensure that we teach them the basics of responsible pet ownership. If we teach our children how to care for a pet dog that is almost entirely dependent on us for survival, then perhaps that will, in some small way, prepare them for their eventual role as parents themselves.

6

Owning More than One Dog

Owning more than one dog is about ten times as difficult as owning only one dog in the same household and we can trace a great number of behaviour problems back to the way two dogs will interact with one another when housed under the same roof. Sometimes it is the reason behind acquiring two dogs that is at the root of the problem. Why should anyone want to own more than one dog, and what are the advantages and disadvantages of multiple dog ownership?

The most popular reason for acquiring a second dog is in the belief that it will keep the first dog company and act as a playmate to relieve boredom. Typically the first dog starts to become a nuisance and begins to chew things every time it is left alone in the house and so a second dog is purchased, usually with the result that the poor owner ends up with two dogs that chew the house to pieces when left.

A second dog is sometimes purchased in an attempt to improve the behaviour of a nervous dog, hoping that the new acquisition will bring it out of its shell. This usually results in, at best, two nervous dogs, or worse, one dog that remains nervous and the other, seeing its role as the nervous dog's protector, becoming increasingly aggressive towards people and/or other dogs.

Most people who are engaged in some form of competitive sport with their dogs own more than one dog, as discussed in Chapter 1, Why Own a Dog? Dogs kept for competitive purposes are very often housed in kennels with two or more sharing a kennel and run, and while this is fine for an older dog, it can cause a number of problems for a very young dog.

Second dogs are sometimes bought with the express purpose of breeding litters of puppies, in which case the second dog will be the opposite sex to the first. This type of ownership is almost exclusively confined to pedigree dogs, particularly those in vogue at the time.

Of course, there are owners who acquire a second dog simply because they enjoy the company of the dog that they presently own and so they purchase a second dog so that, as the first dog grows older, they will never be without the company of a dog in the family.

Let's now examine the effect of a second dog arriving into a house where there is already an older dog that is past maturity.

The young puppy is taken away from its litter-mates, with whom it has already built up a very strong relationship, and arrives at its new home where it feels worried about entering this new environment. There are other people available and, of course, another dog for company. It will immediately relate to the other dog rather than its new owners. Over the next few weeks the relationship between the two dogs will strengthen, often to the point of the younger dog becoming far more interested in playing with the other dog than it is in playing with its owners. The contact that the owners have with the puppy becomes increasingly concerned with correcting bad behaviour such as chewing, house soiling, etc. We now rapidly reach a point where the puppy takes more notice of the older dog than it takes of its owners because interactions with other dogs are generally pleasant while the owners, in the dog's eyes, become mildly unpleasant because of the discipline they try to impose. The good social contact through play that will build a relationship is now becoming the responsibility of the other dog. If the owners try to encourage the puppy to play with a toy, it will not be particularly interested. If the owners throw the toy, the pup will pick it up and take it to the other dog to play with, excluding the owner from the game. Once the pup starts to exclude its owners from games it also starts to exclude them from its life. Rules under which it plays games are dictated by the puppy and the older dog and the owner loses all control of these games, and therefore begins to lose control of the puppy. Any attempts to stop the pup from playing, and attempts either to enforce control or to administer correction result in the pup running to the older dog for comfort. When exercised outside the house the young pup will follow the older dog rather than the owner, and all its interaction with other dogs or people it may meet will be influenced by the games and contact it has had with the older dog. If the young dog is taken out by itself without the company of the other dog at the age of around seven months, and is approached by a person or another dog, it will often become agitated and appear uneasy as it is unable to cope with the situation without the reassuring presence of the other dog. This is why the commonest breed show problem dog that I see, related to aggression or ring shyness, is the younger of more than one dog living in the same environment. That dog has built up a relationship with another dog and cannot cope with any stress while in the company of its owner, with whom it has little or no relationship at all. The owner, in fact, is viewed in the same manner as a piece of furniture.

The problem of correcting bad behaviour also becomes more difficult when two or more dogs are owned, simply because any verbal correction applied to the puppy for its misdemeanours will also be inflicted on the older dog as it will be confused at to just who is in trouble. Just suppose that you arrive home to find that the carpet has been chewed. If you apply the popular 'Who did that' phrase to the puppy then it is likely that your older dog will start to tremble because of its prior association with the tone of your voice. Praising and rewarding either dog for good behaviour will create an interaction between them which will again often exclude the owner. In order to socialise and train a young dog correctly it is important that the relationship between dog and owner is stronger than the younger dog's bond with the other dog in the family. If the owner takes the responsibility for education, mainly through games, rather than leaving this to the other dog, then problems can be minimised. Take a look at the games played between a puppy and an older dog and we get several clues as to future behaviour.

If you allow your young dog unrestricted and unsupervised access to an older dog then it is inevitable that the younger one will want to play all the same games that it played with its litter-mates. These games will consist mainly of chasing and wrestling, which become very enthusiastic on the pup's part.

During the game the pup starts to bite the older dog around the neck and ears which, if the older dog is of a very soft nature, it will tolerate. The owners do nothing to stop these games and they quickly develop to the point where the puppy will not leave the older dog alone when it is feeling playful. The bites become harder and the puppy may actually start to break the skin of the older dog and start to growl and bare its teeth in play in a similar manner to a pup that has been allowed to play at biting its owner's hands. By the time it is old enough to go out to exercise areas with its owners (with whom, you will remember, it does not play) it will become excited at the sight of other dogs and will want to play with them. Its approach towards other dogs and the games it will play with them will now be influenced by the games it has played with the older dog. Most other dogs it meets will accept the fact that it is still a puppy and will tolerate its bullying behaviour to a certain extent. As the pup grows it becomes obsessed with playing with other dogs when exercised and will often cry and whine when restrained on the lead if there are any other dogs about. The owner quite rightly believes that the young dog wants only to play with the other dogs, but we know by now the type of biting, wrestling games that it finds exciting and wants to play. When it gets to about seven months of age there will come a time when it will approach another dog in the manner to which it is accustomed, and the other dog will no longer see a puppy but will see a maturing dog who is rapidly becoming a threat and will attempt to deal with that threat by using aggression. The problem is that the young dog has probably never lost a game of aggression and is now perfectly well equipped to defend itself, having spent the whole of its life practising its fighting techniques on the older dog.

After this first serious confrontation, the owners will be aware of a change in their young dog's behaviour which they often find puzzling. The dog will still get excited when it sees other dogs and will give the appearance of wanting to play, but when it is allowed off the lead it will approach the other dog and will quickly attack it before it has a chance to weigh up the situation. The owner is soon left in no doubt as to the dog's intentions because, after a few repetitions, the young dog will chase and attack dogs and bitches alike when released to play the aggressive games it has learnt, thanks to its older companion.

It may well be the case that when the puppy was first taken home and it tried to play with the older dog, it was growled or snapped at for its undesirable behaviour. This is where the owner would step in very quickly and chastise the older dog for daring to show aggression to the new pup. The owners unfortunately would not be aware that they are reinforcing the pup's behaviour and so it will quickly learn that the owner will back it up in aggressive games with other dogs. Thus when the owner is present, the pup will learn to growl at and bite the other dog, safe in the knowledge that the older dog dare not retaliate. We now have the problem that as the puppy grows it becomes increasingly aggressive towards other dogs when the owner is present, even though other people can walk it past other dogs without difficulty. This is because it has learned that the owner, who has supported it in games of aggression with other dogs, is on hand to assist it in fighting every dog that comes into sight.

Nervous problems towards people are also generally made worse when a young nervy pup is brought up with another dog that it can relate to, because it never needs to learn to socialise and interact with people other than the owners. It will quite often withdraw into the safe world of its canine companion and becomes what I term a 'canine dog' rather than a 'human dog', that is to say that it learns only the canine set of signals and will be quite comfortable, even friendly, with other dogs but frightened or even aggressive with people that it does not know.

Training also becomes difficult when the young dog prefers to be with an older canine companion as it drastically reduces the effectiveness of positive reinforcement or reward training. Just imagine tying up the older dog to a fence or leaving it in the car while you attempt to train the younger one. Every time the pup obeys a training command and you try to praise it, all it wants to do is run over to the other dog, being almost uninterested in the praise that you have to offer. If you try to regain control by shouting at the young dog or by physically dragging it away from the other dog, this serves only to make you less attractive to your puppy, making the other dog more attractive. The more you try to gain the pup's respect, the more you reinforce the older dog as the more pleasant in the relationship.

If you own two or more dogs and wish to find out whether the young dog's relationship towards you is better than its relationship with your other dog(s), then try this simple test. Leave the older dog at home and take the youngster out for a walk for half an hour or so. When you return home, walk into the house alongside the pup and note whom the older dog greets first. If, when you acquired the older dog, it was the only dog in your household at that time, then it will greet you before turning its attentions towards the young dog. Now reverse the process and leave the young dog in the house while you take the older dog out for a walk. When you arrive home and enter the house as before, then it is more than likely that the young dog will say hello to the older dog before it greets you. If this is the case then in order to correct any behaviour problems, particularly those problems that involve aggression, it is essential that you first improve your relationship with the young dog so that it sees you as the most important member of the family. It is almost useless to attempt to teach correct behaviour to a dog that views its owners as merely incidental to its relationship with the other dog.

If you are contemplating purchasing a puppy and already have an older dog in the family, then observing a few guidelines will make the whole process a great deal easier. First of all you will need to decide whether you want a dog or a bitch. Although a dog and a bitch is undoubtedly the best combination to keep in the same house, you will have to give careful consideration to preventing unwanted litters of puppies by having either the bitch spayed or the dog castrated before breeding age is reached. Two male dogs are the next best combination, although in some specific breeds males have a reputation for not getting along very well together – check with the breed society concerned before making a decision.

Two bitches can usually live together perfectly happily under the same roof, but it has to be said that if you start to have serious problems with two bitches that take a dislike to one another it can often lead to serious injury or even the death of one of them. Two male dogs that start to fight are usually fairly easy to cure (see Chapter 8, Dog/Dog Aggression).

What age should your older dog be before you consider getting a second one? Well, it is best to wait until the original dog is fully mature and reasonably well behaved and under proper control. If your dog is out of control, is difficult to handle or you are experiencing any behaviour problems with it, then you should devote all your time and effort towards improving it rather than considering adding to your problems by getting a second dog.

You should definitely never purchase or even contemplate purchasing two puppies from the same litter. This is almost always doomed to disaster because the two pups will already have such a strong bond between them that it is unlikely, unless you are very experienced or exceedingly lucky, that you will end up with any form of control over either dog's behaviour.

If you already own a dog that is quite dominant, when you go to choose a puppy try to pick one that appears to be submissive (do not confuse submissiveness with nervousness). Conversely, if you already own a submissive dog then it would be better to pick a more dominant puppy because there is less likelihood of friction, related to rank, developing between them as the puppy grows.

For the first six months it is important that the puppy learns to enjoy playing more games with you than it plays with the older dog and that any games it plays with the other dog are not allowed to get out of hand. Do not leave any toys lying around for both dogs to play with and when you produce a toy, make sure that the pup is isolated from the attentions and influence of the other dog. You should also try to ensure that the two dogs sleep apart and have no unsupervised access to one another when you are not there. This does not mean that they cannot be in the same room as one another; all you have to do is purchase a wire mesh indoor kennel into which you can place the pup whenever you have to leave the dogs alone for short periods. It will then still have the company of the older dog but will not be in a position to play any games that may otherwise have got out of hand. If you see the puppy approaching the other dog and trying to play games that involve the use of its teeth, then quickly reprimand it by shaking it by the scruff of the neck in a similar manner to the way its mother would have done. It must learn that it is never allowed to use its teeth on anything but a toy. If the puppy appears to be in a playful mood then it is up to you to play with it yourself so that you are in a position to introduce some education and control into such games. You can allow and encourage correct non-aggressive interaction between the two dogs, such as gentle games that do not involve physical strength, and there is a lot to be gained by allowing gentle play to develop between the two of them when the older dog initiates it. You should never allow your young puppy continually to pester the older dog to play. By the time the pup is seven months of age you should be able to call it away from your other dog, even if it is playing, as it should prefer to play games with you rather than your older, or for that matter any other, dog. Education and training now become much easier because of the bond that you will have built between yourself and the pup through play.

You can now allow the pup to sleep with and spend some time with the other dog unsupervised. The two dogs will now be company for one another but each will prefer to be with and to play with you. The added bonus is that your dog will also have learnt to approach other dogs in a non-aggressive manner that would be very unlikely to be looked upon as threatening by any other dog it may encounter.

Dogs that fight, living in the same household

The behaviour of dogs living within a pack is governed by a dominance hierarchy or pecking order, with each dog's position related to status. This simple fact is usually completely overlooked by most owners who have more than one dog. The subsequent disagreements and fights are usually the result of the owner's ignorance in trying to bring up both dogs as equals instead of accepting that there is no such thing as two dogs in a pack that enjoy equal status. It is for this reason that most owners who experience problems with two dogs in the same household report that the dogs fight only when they, the owners, are present. What often confuses the owners is that the two dogs will often share the same bed at night and can be left alone without problems.

To understand this more fully we will take a look at a common area of conflict that can arise when a young dog is just starting to challenge the older dog for dominance. The older dog is sitting alongside the owner being stroked and the young dog enters the room and stares at the older dog. The older dog takes this stare as a challenge and growls to warn the younger dog away. The owner immediately reinforces the younger dog's position by either physically or verbally chastising the older dog, thus making the younger dog more confident about his status when the owner is present. It is easier to understand if we apply the same logic to two children.

If my youngest son Matthew enters my eldest son Marc's bedroom and starts to play around with his stereo equipment then Marc, being ten years Matthew's senior, will challenge and possibly try to assert his authority over him. If Matthew then comes in to me and tells me that Marc has threatened him and I go storming in and reprimand Marc, I am bound to increase the conflict between them because Matthew will start to take advantage of the fact that Marc is powerless to take control while I am in the house. When I am not present then the problem would probably not arise because both parties know their own respective positions. If, on the other hand, when Matthew came in complaining about Marc's threats I chastised him for entering Marc's bedroom and touching equipment that does not belong to him, end of problem. Matthew would very quickly learn the limitations of his status and territory.

If we apply the same logic to two dogs living under the same roof and reinforce the more dominant dog's status by giving him or her the preferential treatment commensurate with its status, then it is possible to reduce or even eliminate any growing conflict between them. Preferential treatment would simply be things like putting the dominant dog's food bowl down first, patting it on the head first when entering the house, putting on its lead first when going out for exercise, etc., all of which serve to remove the confusion that might otherwise exist in the company of the owners.

The idea of giving one dog preferential treatment may not

appeal to many owners but it is the natural way of life for any dog that lives within a pack and they will readily accept and enjoy living like this rather than go through life under constant conflict with their owners and one another. If you feel sorry for the underdog, there is a saying used among dog owners which is that 'every dog has its day'. This means that there will often come a time when the older dog will have to give up its privileged position as head of the canine part of the family to the younger dog. When this happens, you can make the transition much smoother by transferring your allegiance from the older dog to the younger. This may seem really hard on the older dog but it is a way of avoiding serious confrontations between them. This time comes when the young dog has started to win most of the possession games that it plays with the older dog, and the final takeover comes when the younger dog gains total control of the other dog's sleeping areas.

Controlling two dogs

If you are the one who controls the games your dogs play then you should have little in the way of problems controlling both of your dogs. If, on the other hand, you are unable or unwilling to control both dogs when they are playing then you will be the owner of a pack of dogs that do not really see you as a member at all, and you will be unlikely to influence any control should your dogs, for instance, decide to chase other dogs, people, livestock, etc. If you are unlucky enough to be the owner of two dogs that are dominant over you, particularly if one of them is a nervous dog, you will need to get help fast as everyone in the family and in the community will be at serious risk until you regain individual control of your dogs.

Formal training must always initially be carried out individually until you obtain a good measure of control. You can then, by degrees, introduce the distraction of bringing both dogs together to continue this training. You should remember that if you have carried out the early socialisation process between you and your dogs correctly, *you* will be the greatest distraction around with the result that you will have two dogs that respond to you more than they respond to one another.

The pleasures to be gained from owning more than one dog more than repay the expenditure of time and effort involved, but never underestimate just how much of a contribution you will have to make to the dogs' early education and training.

Finally, if the idea of spending a large amount of time playing with two dogs individually for the first seven months does not appeal to you, then please do not even consider getting a second dog. If you have acquired a second dog as a playmate for your first dog because you yourself do not have the time to play with it, perhaps you should never have owned a dog in the first place.

7

Dog/Human Aggression Problems

This chapter has been written so that you are better able to understand your dog's behaviour and are therefore in a better position to improve any undesirable behaviour that may be present. Although techniques are given for modifying aggressive behaviour, it is important that this is carried out under the expert supervision of your vet or a recognised dog-behaviour consultant to whom your vet may refer you. It is not intended as a do-it-yourself guide to curing problems of canine aggression.

It is interesting to note that when an adult dog actually bites someone, the *site* of the bite wound is usually a good indication of where, when it was a puppy, it was inadvertently taught to bite. Thus a puppy that has been encouraged to bite (or not discouraged from biting) its owner's hands and fingers will focus any aggression towards that region if it starts to become aggressive. Similarly a pup that has been encouraged to bite at its owner's trouser leg will attack the leg area when it matures. Where the owners have played games on the floor and allowed the pup to bite at their hair or have blown into the pup's face to encourage it to snap at them, the maturing dog will concentrate any future attack on that region of the body, often with tragic consequences.

Dominant aggression towards owners and family

Before the behaviour of the dominant dog and the reasons behind his aggression are explained, it is most important to remember that dogs cannot think in the same way we do. All their behaviour is based on instinct and conditioned responses (training), or learnt through trial and error. Throughout the text the dog is referred to as he, but it applies equally to a bitch – this problem is seen in all sizes, breeds and sexes.

Behaviour in the litter

It is as instinctive for puppies to learn 'their place' as it was for them to find a teat and suckle when they were first born. The most dominant puppy will force his way to suckle at the most productive teat between the bitch's hind legs. Because of this he will gain extra weight over his litter-mates and will use this extra strength to make sure he always gets to these teats first. If mum is introduced after a short absence the puppies will all compete for the available milk supply. If a more submissive pup manages to start suckling first, the more dominant pup will quickly push it out of the way, detaching it from the teat. He will also use his extra weight to get into the most comfortable and safest place to sleep, again between the mother's hind legs.

When puppies' senses have developed at approximately four weeks, learning games start between them. The games teach them skills they will need later in life, and are those of wrestling, chasing, killing, mating and, most important of all with regard to the dominant dog, games of strength and possession. The puppies will use any item they are able to carry such as a toy, piece of rag or bedding material. They will all chase and investigate the 'trophy'; one will pick it up and will play chase and tug-of-war with a litter-mate until one gives in, and the winner will then take on another puppy. The chasing and tugging continue until one puppy eventually wins possession of the 'trophy', takes it away and lies down with it. If any of the pups try to regain possession of the toy, they will be either play-bitten or growled at, or the pup who has possession will quickly pick it up and run away. The game is played often, the winner getting more interested in showing his litter-mates just who is strongest and the boss.

At weaning the dominant puppy will often control the greatest area of the feeding bowl, ensuring that he gets the greatest quantity and best quality of food. He is usually the one with his front paws actually in the bowl! (This is why it is wise to have several food bowls when feeding puppies to ensure that they all get their fill, not just the strongest.)

When the puppies get tired and want to rest or sleep, the dominant pup will sleep in any area of the territory it chooses. None of the other pups will be able to move the more dominant one when it is resting, although the dominant pup can easily move any other from their resting area and claim the area for itself whenever it wants to. There are also occasional growls if any of the more submissive puppies roll over in their sleep and disturb the dominant one. The technique of play-biting and using bodily strength to push the other pups out of its desired spot are usually employed to gain control of resting areas.

By the time the dominant puppy is ready to go to his new home he is already confident of his strength, never losing a game, always eating and having his fill first and also having the safest and most comfortable place to sleep.

Behaviour within a pack of dogs

If we place this dominant puppy among a pack of dogs, he once again has to find his position in life and will carefully watch this pack to discover who is pack leader and the general order of the rest of the pack. The ways through which he will learn are the following.

1. The pack leader has a right to eat first.
For example, if one food bowl is put down for eight dogs it will usually be the more dominant ones that get to the food and start to eat first. The others will then approach the bowl and feed. The dog who made the first move will be the pack leader, and if more than one bowl is used and he decides he wants a different bowl after he has started to eat, it is his right to approach another dog's bowl. The more submissive dog will instinctively back off, allowing his leader to eat. The submissive dog will then go to the vacant food bowl. Any reluctance on the submissive member's part will result in a scuffle or fight if necessary. Any member of the pack who dares to approach the pack leader while he is eating will often be growled at or perhaps snapped at.

2.   The pack leader also 'owns' any toys, etc. that the dogs are given.

All the dogs will play with the toy; the pack leader may not necessarily be the first to pick it up if the toy is thrown but he is always the one who ends the game by taking it away and lying next to it. He will either growl at any member who tries to take a toy or pick it up and move it to a safer, easily defended area when he doesn't want them to have it. He has won ownership of the toys through the same games as the puppies in the litter played, i.e. games of tugging and growling over the toy.

3.   The sleeping place of the pack leader is always the safest, most comfortable area within his territory.

He will allow another member of his pack to use his area if he doesn't want it at the time but any approach by him results in the submissive member getting up, allowing his pack leader to lie down. Once again, any uninvited approach will often provoke a growl or snap.

4.   When the pack leader wants grooming he will push himself at the pack members, inviting them to groom him; they will then lick him all over but especially around the face and muzzle.

Once again any member of the pack who tries to touch him without invitation will be repelled either by play-biting the offending dog around the muzzle or front legs, or by growling.

5.   If the pack is under any threat from a human or a dog not from their pack, it is up to the pack leader, as he is the strongest, to chase away any threat.

He is so convinced he is the best one to cope with any threat that he will attack a submissive member of his pack if it tries to get to the threat first.

Our puppy, from watching all the above behaviour, now knows who is pack leader. If he wants that position he has to work his way up the pack order, starting with the weakest, until he is eating first, has the best place to sleep, owns all possessions and guards his territory and pack from danger. He has then taken over as pack leader.

All the above behaviour is instinctive and handed down from the dog's wild ancestors. The most dominant dog and bitch always ate the kill first, slept in the safest area, etc. so that in times of famine or bad winters the strongest breeding pairs survived to breed the next year, producing strong, healthy puppies – survival of the fittest.

The puppy in his new family home

When you take your dominant puppy home, in his eyes he is leaving one pack of animals to arrive in another. Remember, he cannot think in the same way as we can and therefore doesn't see himself as a dog and you as people; we are all animals to him and form a pack.

As when the puppy was put with other dogs, he has to find out who is pack leader in this new human pack. Within the first forty-eight hours he will have found out by watching family meals. In the pup's eyes it is the most dominant member of the household who eats first. Quite often the puppy is shown by a family member where the pack leader sleeps within the pack's territory, i.e. the bedrooms and other resting areas such as the living room. He is almost always given toys that he is allowed to play with when he wants.

If the puppy wants to be leader of this pack he must go through a pattern of behaviour with members of the family who are prepared to take notice of him and play games with him. That usually includes every member of the immediate family, for who can resist the appeals of a young puppy? These games and behaviour, if handled wrongly by the owners (and they usually are), will eventually elevate him to his desired position. He then rules the whole family, house, garden, car, etc.

How dominance develops

As family meals are being prepared the puppy paces the floor, cries or perhaps nudges his food bowl. The owners will then often feel sorry for the puppy and, believing that it is really hungry and incapable of waiting for a few minutes while they eat their own meal, will put down the pup's food so that they can have some peace. What the pup is doing is conditioning his owners to offer him food first. Note the word *offered*. He may not eat his meal straight away but the fact that he has been given his food first will satisfy one condition for his climb to being pack leader.

The puppy plays games with its toys with members of the family prepared to play. He loves the game of tug-of-war: the harder you pull, the harder he pulls. The game isn't necessarily played with a pull toy; he can do just as well with a ball or squeaky toy that you have to struggle to get off him. He becomes obsessed as he wins more and more games of strength. He will leap up and down most agitatedly if the toy is taken from him. By fourteen to sixteen weeks of age he may start to growl playfully while tugging. The growling is further encouraged by unwitting owners who praise him and make growling noises back. The games finish in one of two ways: either the puppy decides he has had enough and takes away the toy, or the fed-up owner refuses to play any more and encourages the puppy to take the toy away.

Sometimes the owner will keep the toy until the puppy settles down. The toy is then put back on the floor or in the puppy's bed so that the puppy still has access to the toy. It is extremely rare for any dog to growl at his owners unless he has played this seemingly harmless game!

A game often played by owners with the puppy is this: as the puppy is lying near its toy the owner will sneak up, saying something like 'I'm going to get your toy,' and pretends to snatch it away from him. The puppy's immediate response is to snatch up his toy and run off with it to a safe place. All great fun!

Now let us look at the way the puppy sees these games. We all learn from the games we play and the puppy is no exception; in fact, the young of all animals need to play to learn skills necessary later in life. The puppy, from these games, has learnt a few valuable lessons. Because these games of strength always end with the puppy having possession of a toy, he thinks he has won all the games and therefore is stronger than the people who have played with him. Also he has learnt to growl at his owners. He now knows if he wants something that you also want he has only to growl in order to keep it. You have taught him that. When you were playing and he growled, he always got the toy. The game of 'sneak up' you played with him has taught him another lesson, *viz* if you want something he has, his best course of action is to get up and run off with it before you snatch it from him.

An extension of this game is discovered accidentally by the puppy at approximately seventeen weeks of age. The puppy is obsessed with showing his pack how strong he is and pushes his toys in people's faces if necessary to get them to play. One day all efforts are ignored by everyone, so the puppy drops his toy in disgust and wanders round. By chance he will pick up some item lying around the room such as a pair of socks, a slipper or a tea towel, and WOW – suddenly everyone wants to play with him and quite a game of chase begins (he has already learnt to run off with his possessions). At first the owner manages to catch the pup and remove the item that it was not allowed to have, but that only encourages him to play even harder the next time. The stealing problem gets worse – he goes behind or underneath furniture to make it harder to get to him and games of tug-of-war will be played with his bounty. One day as he gets older he will put into practice his growling lesson and will growl over the article, much to the amazement of his owners. But this is what you taught him to do over the toy. Eventually no one dares take the bounty off him; he is usually bribed with a biscuit or the promise of a walk by dangling his lead in front of him. This only further rewards his stealing and growling.

When this stage is reached another condition is satisfied: he has possessions which no one is strong enough to take from him.

As mentioned earlier, the new puppy is often shown the pack leader's sleeping area or will find it through his explorations of the house. He may already have taken over the pack leader's sleeping area because his howls, pitiful cries or destruction when kept overnight in the kitchen had led his owners to allow him upstairs to get some peace, because he is lonely, etc. If he wants to be a pack leader he must gain control of the bedroom. If he is allowed to sleep on the bed he may even growl when the owners turn in their sleep and disturb him. If he hasn't achieved his need to sleep in the bedroom he will try to get in at every opportunity and will eventually growl when he is made to get off the bed or out of the room. If he is allowed to sleep in the bedroom, especially if he sleeps on the bed, another condition has been satisfied for his elevation to pack leadership.

An extension to the bedroom area and bed is the furniture downstairs. A common trait is for the puppy immediately to jump into a chair vacated by a family member who gets up to make a cup of tea. There are other chairs available but the puppy wants that particular one, not because it is warm but because he is reinforcing his ownership of it. If the dog is small enough to share a chair he will jump up and push and stretch until the owner is sitting right on the edge or gets up to move to another chair.

This dominant puppy loves to be touched and petted: he will go through all sorts of behaviour to get attention. Try to touch him when he doesn't want to be touched, e.g. while he is resting, eating or when you want to groom or generally check him over, and you get a totally different reaction. The very young puppy will try to turn grooming and handling into a game by wriggling and running away, which then turns into a chase game with the potential groomer. As the puppy gets older he will tug on the towel, bite the brush or snap at the air. If this doesn't stop the attempted grooming session, he will growl. Owners then start to get frightened or find it too much trouble and give up all attempts to groom him. But this same puppy who will not accept such handling will always allow himself be petted when he goes through his attention-seeking behaviour. This touching on demand concludes all the conditions of pack leadership. The conditions may not be satisfied in the order just described, but now our growing puppy eats or is offered food first, sleeps in the bedroom or tries to get in at any chance, believes he is the strongest, and knows how to keep people away from him by growling and thereby hang on to his possessions; in other words, he is pack leader. His instincts tell him he owns the house, possessions in it, garden and pack and it is up to him to protect his pack and territory. He will also keep his pack firmly in line, often becoming agitated if one of the family leaves the house, even though he has the company of others.

Obedience-wise the maturing puppy is not very well behaved. It is difficult to get him into the down (submissive) position or this can be achieved only after a struggle, and any commands are carried out in the dog's own time, if at all, and not immediately, as should happen. Smacking has no effect on his behaviour. In fact, if the dog is chastised by its owner, the aggression becomes worse. Remember, he has never lost a game of aggression in his life. Shouts of 'shut up', etc. when he is barking and guarding his territory will be ignored. No pack leader worth his salt takes any notice of submissive members of his pack. Quite often these dogs will not allow themselves to be touched or grabbed by the collar or back of the neck. It can be a struggle to get the lead attached to his collar; he has learnt that when he is on the lead he is under your control. This is the one battle that nearly all owners do win; the puppy is put on a lead and no matter how much fuss he creates he will eventually learn he has to go where the owner wants. He will understand that when he is on the lead the owner is generally stronger, even though he will usually pull on the lead against the owner.

As the puppy starts to mature he gains more and more confidence and the situations where previously he growled become even more fierce – he really means the growls and now also snaps the air. At maturity (age of maturity depends on the breed – the bigger the breed the older the dog will be), the age at which he will bite, given the right set of circumstances he will turn on each of the family, starting with the ones he sees as the most submissive.

Places/times most likely to get aggressive reactions

1.   Probably top of the list is the owner's bed. The owner gets up to go to the toilet during the night and on his return the dog attacks when the owner tries to get back into bed, or if the dog is pushed in an attempt to get him down off the bed. Sometimes, all that is necessary in extreme cases is for the owner to walk into the bedroom while the dog is on the bed. Similar patterns occur with the furniture downstairs. The dog will have certain areas, including his basket if he has one, scattered around the house where he likes to relax. Trying to pet him while he is in these particular areas or just walking past can provoke aggression.

2.   His food, including chew bones, is important to him and he could be aggressive not only over his food but over any food, where the food is kept, the food-preparing area (kitchen), or even show aggression when sitting next to his owner when anyone approaches while the owner is eating. In extreme cases, walking past food while he is near or even walking into the kitchen when he is in there will often result in some sort of aggression.

3.   He will also possibly bite instead of the usual growl over something he has stolen and taken to a safe area, usually behind or under furniture. The owner has to get down to the dog's level and stretch out his hand to retrieve the article and it is an invitation to the dog to bite the hand to keep it away. Remember the games of tug that taught him to growl when he thought you were trying to remove something from his mouth?

4.   As mentioned earlier, this type of dog does not like to be touched or grabbed by the back of the neck and if he is suddenly grabbed to check him he could turn and bite. Because of this sensitive area, sometimes the action of putting on his lead will provoke aggression. Another reason for this behaviour is because when on the lead this big, strong, confident dog is totally under your control. (Remember, you won that particular battle.) Another possible trait is that the dog will guard his lead. He could bite at an approach because he is guarding his lead, because his lead, which he associates with pleasant walks, is another of his possessions.

5.   Another reasonably common aggressive situation is when the dog is checked by his owner for barking at some threat, e.g. someone knocking at the door or barking at another dog. The dog sees it as his responsibility to see off threats and will put in its place any weaker member of the pack who dares to intervene – in this case it will be the human member of the family who has tried to check him.

6.   Grooming doesn't often lead to an attack because, after all the growls and struggles when the dog was younger, the family have usually given up trying and the dog is sent off to the local dog groomer who normally has no trouble at all from the dog (the dog is off its territory and doesn't know the strength of the groomer). The crunch can come when the dog needs home medical care, wounds cleaned, drops in the ears, eyes, etc. The owners try harder to get the dog to accept this handling and may get bitten in the process, or the dog doesn't get its medication.

7.   This dog really loves to be touched and stroked and will demand to be petted, pestering until he gets what he wants. Often the owner doesn't even realise he is petting the dog,

because the dog has got him so well conditioned. His way of showing that he has had enough or he doesn't want touching because he is resting, etc. is through showing aggression, and the aggression is often a growl followed by a bite.

If you own a dog that has become dominant with you, you now understand him and realise he is normal in every way. In the wild he would be the survivor, but in the family situation his behaviour is anti-social to say the least. His previous growls, snaps or bites for 'no reason' would have had a reason, if you think back. Was he near food, his toy, resting in a favourite place, had enough petting, etc.?

In order to reverse his behaviour it is necessary to reverse his position in the pack and put him where all dogs belong, *right at the bottom of the pack*. He will always see one member of the household as most dominant; this doesn't matter as long as he realises *everyone* is above him. If you own other dogs it doesn't matter where he finishes up in regard to them; let the dogs sort out their own relative positions and don't interfere too much unless absolutely necessary.

Controlling the dominant dog

Behaviour alteration is divided into five stages which, with a young dog, can be implemented at weekly intervals or with an older dog at fortnightly intervals. The idea behind making these changes a week or fortnight apart is to prevent the dog becoming more aggressive when he suddenly realises that you are demoting him to the bottom of the pack. Making each change after he has accepted the previous one usually ensures that the dog will slowly and gradually come to accept his new status. I would strongly recommend that the programme for reducing dominance is carried out only under the supervision of an experienced dog-behaviour consultant or vet, to reduce the possibility of misinterpretation by either owner or dog. If you are happy about your adult dog's behaviour then it is unwise and unfair on the dog to instigate any of the mentioned changes. The programme is to be used only to allow the owner of a dominant and possibly aggressive dog to regain control in a way the dog can understand. If you own a young dog that has started to show signs of dominance, you may like to consider toys, food and grooming as a means of preventing the dog becoming increasingly dominant as it matures.

Important: Ignore the dog as much as possible during the first three stages. For example, if he puts his head in your lap or pushes against you to get you to stroke him, turn your back on him or, if necessary, get up and go into the next room, closing the door and leaving him on his own. Do not push him away or shout at him as he will then have achieved his objective, i.e. getting your attention. It is very hard for most pet-dog owners to do this, but the object of it all is to reserve all praise and petting for the behaviour you want from your dog later in the course of treatment, for example coming when called, sitting on command, etc. Because your dog is not now getting praise constantly for doing nothing, it will mean so much more to him when he gets praise for doing something you want him to do.

Do not give in to his demands for attention. It is not his right; he must earn your affection by altering his behaviour to please you.

Stage 1

Remove all items your dog is likely to steal by putting them out of his reach. They will be replaced at a later stage. For the rest of his life he owns no toys – you do! So pick up all toys and keep them where he has no access to them. Play with him as much as you want (young children should play with your dog under supervision of an adult). Tug-of-war games should be played with you winning the games more often than not but always ultimately retaining possession of the toy. Put the toy on the arm of the chair and tell him to leave. Enforce this command by using the lead to hold the dog away from the toy if necessary. Games start and end when *you* want; make a habit of finishing when the dog is still keen and then put the toy away to where the dog cannot gain access to it. This ensures that the family now win all games of strength and possession.

Stage 2

Ignore your dog as much as possible. Alter the dog's feeding pattern. Your dog for the rest of his life must eat after the family have eaten. Do this in the following way: mix the dog's food while preparing a family meal. Let the dog know that his meal is ready at the same time as the family meal is ready by allowing him to watch both meals being prepared. Place his food out of his reach and have your meal, allowing him to watch; tie him up if he is a nuisance at the table. When the family have finished and the table has been cleared, offer the dog his meal, pick up any uneaten food after fifteen minutes and do not give any further food until the next meal-time.

Do not give titbits. Food that you have been eating should not be given directly but put into his bowl and given to him later. In a dog pack the dominant dog will take food from a weaker member while he is eating. You will be encouraging him to he dominant if you allow him to take titbits from you or members of your family. This is why dominant dogs tend to stare at their owners while they are eating, in an attempt to intimidate them into offering food.

Stage 3
Ignore your dog as much as possible. For the rest of his life he must sleep as far away from the bedrooms as possible and be denied further access. You can move him gradually if necessary, outside the bedroom door on to the landing then at the foot of the stairs, etc., until he is where you decide that he must sleep. He must never set foot inside any of the bedrooms again, even while beds are being made or the carpet vacuumed. The doors are now firmly shut against him. Preventing him from gaining access to the bedrooms and, if possible, from the upstairs part of the house will retain an exclusive sleeping area for you and the rest of your family, which helps to reduce the dog's status within the pack. If you have difficulty in getting the dog to accept sleeping away from the bedroom, then read the section Destruction when left alone (page 148 in Chapter 9, Other Behaviour Problems).

Stage 4
If when you took all the dog's toys away in Stage 1 the dog started to steal other possessions and you put everything that he was likely to steal out of his reach, you can now replace these items. Whenever anyone is in the house attach a ten-foot length of lightweight line to his collar. The line is allowed to trail behind him wherever he goes and is used *gently* for any control needed. For example, if he steals something and runs away,

particularly if he gets under or behind something with the article, do not chase him but merely go and pick up the end of the line and gently pull the dog towards you. Remove the article from his mouth, using a taste deterrent if necessary (Bitter Apple, etc.), and then praise him for giving it to you. If he gets on to your chair and you want to sit there yourself, then pick up the end of the line and make him get off, remembering to praise and fuss him for obeying you. As you have ignored him for the first three stages the fuss and attention he receives for doing what you want him to do will mean a great deal to him and he will want to repeat his good behaviour in order to receive your affection and attention. Do not issue any instruction to your dog while in the house for the next two weeks unless you have the end of the line in your hand. This puts your dog in a position where he cannot refuse to obey your commands and it will dramatically improve your control over him. Always ensure that you remember to praise him well when he behaves in a way that pleases you. It is also a good idea to reinforce the idea in his mind that he does not own anything at all by calling him away from resting places such as his bed or the rug in front of the fire and taking his place there yourself for a few minutes. If he is lying on the floor in your way you must get out of the habit of walking around him and start making him get up and move out of your way. You will need to use the line less and less to get him to obey you on the first command and he should be quite happy to do so as obeying and pleasing you brings the reward of attention.

The line is removed after two weeks but will need to be replaced at any time in the future if the dog starts to regress. It must be removed at night or whenever the dog is left unattended because of the danger of it tangling around something.

Stage 5

If you have not been shown how to groom your dog by the breeder, then contact a professional groomer, breeder, vet, training instructor or behaviour consultant and ask for a lesson on grooming and handling. They will show you how to restrain your dog by fastening its lead to a fixed object, which leaves you both hands free to groom and handle the dog and manipulate it into the positions that you want (see the section on Grooming and handling (page 61) in Chapter 3, Surviving the First Six Months.

e: If the correct
ting rituals are
rved then there are
om any problems. Note
both dogs are careful
void eye contact and
past one another

t: How not to greet
her dog! This is often
result of owning more
a one dog and allowing
sing games to get out of
d

Providing one dog shows immediate signs of submission then things rarely develop into an actual fight and the owners can regain control

A dog that has played lots of chasing games as a puppy is quite likely to chase joggers etc., unless the games have been played under the control of the owner

Above left: A dog that barks constantly when left can seriously damage relationships between owners and neighbours and yet it is a fairly simple problem to correct

Above right: Fear, whether real or imaginary, can be linked to a disagreeable experience

Below: A dog that barks in the car can prove very difficult to correct because of a number of possible reasons behind this behaviour. Before you can correct the problem you must first establish the cause

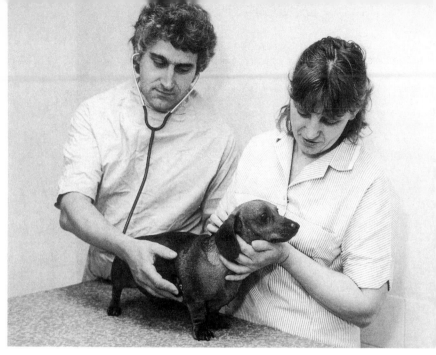

If behaviour problems arise then it is important that your vet gives your dog a thorough examination first to eliminate physical causes

A behavioural adviser will want to speak to the whole family in order to devise a suitable treatment programme

Grooming then needs to be carried out each day with all the family becoming involved. It is important that children are allowed to groom the dog only when the parents can manage it easily, and even then there must be an adult in supervision.

Always follow the grooming sessions with something pleasant like a walk, his dinner or a game with a toy. This teaches your dog to accept being touched and handled on your terms, making the whole process of physically handling the dog much easier for all concerned.

As you will realise, you are, through the games that you have played and rules you have made, putting your previously dominant dog firmly in his place. He should instinctively understand all of this as he has played the same games and set all of the rules with you since you brought him home. He now eats last, sleeps on the fringe of the pack, plays games according to the rules that you have now set, attention and petting are no longer his by right and he has learnt to accept being handled on your terms.

As he now has to rely on you for all the things that are important to him in life, you should find that, as well as the aggression ceasing, he becomes a more biddable dog that goes through life wanting to please you.

In addition to carrying out all of the above stages, the following should help to reduce your dog's dominance more quickly.

1. Avoid situations that are likely to provoke aggression. Every successful confrontation the dog has with you (for example if the dog growls at you when you try to take something away from it and you withdraw your hand and let him keep the item) will increase his dominance and slow down the whole programme.
2. Do not issue a command unless you are in a position to make sure that he obeys it.
3. Do not let him take up dominant positions like jumping up with his paws on your lap while you are sitting down.
4. Do not allow him to proceed ahead of you through doorways, upstairs or into new situations.
5. After you have gone through Stages 1–3 give your dog daily obedience sessions. Join your local dog-training club

where you will be shown how to improve your training techniques and increase your control over your dog.

Aggression towards people other than its owners

By far the most common aggression problem towards people other than the dog's owners is nervous aggression. To understand more about nervous aggression we shall examine the two most common causes.

Although there may be genetic influences on the dog's temperament, by far the biggest influence on a young dog's developing behaviour is environmental. It follows, then, that from birth to the age at which most puppies are placed in their new homes the main effect on their behaviour is going to be learnt from their mother. If mum herself is in any way nervous then her natural protective behaviour towards her puppies will make her even more apprehensive about complete strangers coming into the territory near to her puppies. She will pace back and forth in an agitated manner, often with hackles raised. The puppies will instinctively recognise the fear their mother is exhibiting and will huddle together in a corner, frightened by the whole experience. Each and every time mum feels threatened by the approach of a person she behaves in an aggressive manner, often by racing at the intruder, barking furiously, in order to protect herself and her puppies. The puppies will learn two things from their exposure to this type of behaviour: first, they will become extremely suspicious of strangers, and secondly they will note how effective their mother was in dealing with such a threat by using aggression and intimidation. The longer it stays with its mother, the greater the chances of the puppy copying this type of undesirable behaviour.

When it is eventually placed in a new home it will settle down with its new owners within a few weeks and become more and more secure within the home environment. By the time it is around sixteen weeks of age the owners will start to notice a change in its behaviour towards people it meets in the house. It will start hiding behind furniture when people arrive, only peeking out to give the occasional bark at the person who is placing it under stress. It is here that the unwitting owners start to take a hand in 'socialising' the pup by insisting that it comes out to meet people. This is usually accomplished by picking up the puppy and taking it over to the person it is frightened of, thereby increasing its fear of them. Because it has been deprived of a safe place to hide, the growing pup starts to modify its behaviour by anticipating that it is going to be made to approach the person and so it will pace back and forth, not daring actually to go up and make contact with the person it is frightened of. If, at any time during this encounter, the person makes any sudden, unexpected moves or leans towards the pup, making eye contact, then it will put into effect the lungeing/barking technique so ably taught by its mother. The first time this happens it will startle both the owner and the visitor, but the reward the pup gets is instantaneous – the offending person jumps back, withdrawing their hands. After this stage is reached the behaviour starts rapidly to get worse until the young dog is barking furiously whenever anyone comes to the house whom it does not meet on a regular basis. When exercised outside, the pup will probably walk through a crowd without too much difficulty, but if only one person approaches, particularly if they make eye contact, the pup will try to hide behind its owner's legs. The response of most owners is to pull the dog forward towards the person it is frightened of, usually saying something like 'Come on, don't be silly, they are not going to hurt you.' After a few repetitions the dog will have learnt to do exactly what the unwitting owner has taught it – lunge forward because there is no escape route available. Once again, as soon as the young dog starts to do this it will immediately be receiving two huge rewards; one is that the other person will quickly step backwards and the other is that the owner will pull the dog away. This is exactly the reward that the dog's behaviour is designed to achieve.

The advice that is usually given by well-meaning friends at this stage is to check the dog hard and shout 'no' at it every time this happens. This, of course, never works because it does absolutely nothing to remove the dog's fear of strangers. Castrating a male dog or spaying a bitch will also have no effect on curing a nervous aggression problem, i.e. it will not make the dog less frightened of people and it may conceivably make it more frightened.

The thing that most people find hard to understand is that the dog is almost always more aggressive outside when it is on the lead. That is because it knows it is unable to escape from threats and therefore has to keep people away at all costs, whilst when exercising off the lead it has the opportunity of avoiding contact with people it is worried about.

As the dog matures its problem invariably worsens, usually due to ignorance on the owner's part, and it will now start lungeing at some people without warning as they walk past, occasionally making contact with their arms or hands. The dog usually becomes bonded closer and closer with its owners as it becomes more and more wary of strangers, and most owners are then under the impression that the dog is protecting them. Unless the dog is in fact dominant with the owners, then it is not protecting them at all; it is protecting itself, and they just happen to be there with the dog at the time.

I should mention that if you have a dog that is nervous and aggressive with other people and very dominant with you, it is important that the dominance problem is corrected first.

Looking at things from the dog's point of view, if someone approaches, the way of avoiding confrontation would be to lunge forward to remove the threat. If the owner then starts to show aggression towards the dog, then the end result will simply be that the dog will start to behave aggressively much earlier. The further away he keeps the threat, the less is the likelihood of the owner getting aggressive. This also explains why the dog will often be much worse when it is with one particular member of the family; it is usually the one who has been the most aggressive towards him in these encounters. Muzzling a nervous, aggressive dog can often make the behaviour much worse as the dog will feel even more trapped and unable to control the situation.

Nervous aggression, the effect of early environmental conditions

A puppy that has been kept with litter brothers and sisters beyond the age of sixteen weeks and has not had the opportunity to meet either the conditions with which it will be expected to cope, or people in the world away from the small, enclosed environment in which it has been kept, will usually grow up to be a dog which exhibits more than one category of nervous behaviour. The longer it has the company of other dogs the less likely it will be ever to relate to people. Confining a puppy in a kennel and run with its litter-mates or even another, unrelated dog, will bring about a situation where the pup becomes a trembling wreck whenever it is parted from the other dog or taken away from the security of its home. If it is re-homed into an environment where it has the company of another dog it will immediately bond itself to that in preference to the owners (see Chapter 6, Owning More than One Dog). You then rapidly get a situation where the young dog seems reasonably friendly in its own home, particularly when the other dog is nearby, but when it is taken away from home for exercise without the other dog it becomes stressed and unable to come to terms with the situation in which it finds itself. Most pet dogs pull on the lead when taken out for a walk because they enjoy free exercise, but a feature of this type of nervous dog is that it will pull hardest when it is heading back towards the security of its home or car. Take it in the show ring and it will not let the judge anywhere near it, either continually backing away or growling/lungeing to keep the judge at bay. This is in fact the most common breed show problem I am asked to advise on. What the owner finds hard to accept is that the poor dog is put into a position where he is placed under conditions of severe stress and in that situation is with a person he has absolutely no relationship with – the owner.

If the puppy is taken away from the company of other dogs when it is over the age of sixteen weeks and placed into a new home without another dog present, it will usually bond strongly with one person and then withdraw into its own small world, into which very few people will be allowed. It will often become totally obsessed with that person and will tolerate the presence of other members of the family but will rarely attempt to interact with them. It will also generally be friendly with any other dogs it may meet but will hate people approaching either inside the house or on the occasions when it is taken out.

Puppies never start off with nervous, aggressive problems; they may start off as nervous, but the aggression comes later, dependent on the owner and the attitudes of the people the dog will encounter.

In order to improve the behaviour of the nervous or nervous aggressive dog it is important to understand that if the dog has accepted *you* as being a friendly person to be with, then it has to be possible to transfer that attitude to other people. If, on the other hand, you have owned a dog for several weeks and it is still worried about you, then I would certainly not be particularly optimistic about the possibility of curing it of being worried about other people.

If you think back to the time when you acquired your nervous puppy or young dog, how did you get him to accept and enjoy your company? You will have built up a relationship based on fulfilling the dog's requirements to play, eat and socialise with another pack animal. It is by adopting a similar approach that you can start the process of reducing the dog's fear of and aggression towards people. The programme is given in stages and it is important that each stage is carried out in turn and you do not move on to the next stage until the previous one has been successfully accomplished. I would strongly recommend that the programme is used under the guidance of a dog-behaviour consultant or vet.

Stage 1
If there are other dogs in the household then your problem dog must be separated from them for the next six months. Separation simply means no playing together, no sleeping together and no unsupervised access to one another. They can be together whenever there is anyone present to supervise, but the idea is to prevent the dogs from playing games together. This will reduce any bonds that your 'problem' dog may have formed with other dogs, allowing you to rebuild a bond between yourself and the dog initially and then ultimately a bond between the dog and other people.

For the first two weeks find a favourite toy that your dog likes to play with, produce it and invite the dog to play with it whenever it gets naturally excited. This would mean that when you get up in the morning and the dog is pleased to see you, produce the toy and play. Remember that, because it now sleeps by itself, away from the company of other dogs, it will be especially pleased to see you and more likely to play with the toy. If you do not own another dog and your dog sleeps in the bedroom then it would be advisable to move it out of the bedroom for the duration of the programme. Other times to play would be if the dog gets excited when it knows it is going to be fed; when you enter the house after a short absence; when you take it out in the car, etc. The idea is to link all excitement with a game with the toy. A dog is much more likely to play with a toy when it is excited, and because you have excluded other dogs from the games (if you own more than one dog), your dog will become more interested in playing with you. Play only as long as the dog remains enthusiastic, always stopping before it gets bored by putting the toy away out of sight in a place where the dog has no access to it.

As each day passes the dog should become more interested in the toy because that is now the only way that it can play any games. By the time two weeks have elapsed, if you produce the toy you should get an immediate, excitable response from your dog even if there is nothing going on to excite him. Once this condition is satisfied, you can move on to Stage 2.

Stage 2

Move the toy to a visible position near the door where most people would enter the house. The toy must remain inaccessible to the dog even though it will be able to see it. For the next two weeks, every time anyone in the immediate family enters the house they must ignore the dog's attempts to jump up and otherwise try to gain attention and go straight over to where the toy is positioned, produce it and invite the dog to play. All other games in the house must now stop. When the stage is reached where anyone in the family entering the house results in the dog positioning itself away from the door and near the toy in anticipation of playing with it, you can go on to Stage 3.

Stage 3

Tease the dog with the toy on occasions through the day but do not let it actually touch it. The toy is still kept in a visible position near the door for the dog to see. Now arrange for one or two friends whom the dog knows and is relatively friendly with to call. If you are worried about the situation then place the dog on a lead, but do not hold on to it. The lead is there only as a safety measure in cases where the dog has a history of aggression. Tell the person to enter and immediately go to where the toy is kept, without looking at or speaking to the dog. They should then remove the toy and throw it past the dog. Allow the dog to run after and play with the toy, using as much encouragement as you can. Take the toy from the dog and throw it back to your visitor, who is then instructed to walk past the dog, again without looking at or speaking to it. After a few paces they should throw the toy again and allow the dog to play for half a minute or so. This process is repeated until they are seated, whereupon they are instructed to ignore the dog but to hold on to the toy. Any attempt the dog makes to approach in a friendly manner should result in the toy being thrown for it. The dog's focus of attention should now be firmly fixed on the toy and not on the person, so even if the visitor looks directly at

Favourite toy positioned near the entrance for visitors to use when they come into the house

the dog it will not be aware of the fact. When your visitor gets up to leave they must be told to ignore the dog again and go quietly to the door. Before going out of the door tell them to throw the toy one last time and then as the dog goes to pick it up, they can leave and you can take the toy from the dog and replace it in position near the door once again. If you can get a number of different friends whom the dog knows to visit you and do the same for two to four weeks, you should begin to see a marked improvement in the dog's overall behaviour. Remember that it is important to ensure that the majority of play now comes from other people and not from you or other members of your family. If you all still play with the dog then this will tend to reduce its desire to play with other people.

Stage 4
Now get as many people as you can to come to the house, and repeat the process, preferably using people with whom the dog is unfamiliar. If your dog likes to go out for walks then you can reduce the amount of times you take it out and get other people to take it instead. It also helps if you now start getting other people to come in and mix up its food before allowing them to feed it.

Stage 5
Once the dog is reliable and relaxed inside the house you can start to improve its behaviour towards people you meet outside. To do this you will need completely to stop playing all games in the house and take a toy out with you when you exercise your dog. Find a quiet spot where there are no distractions and tease the dog with the toy before encouraging him to play. You must be patient, as it is quite possible that your dog will feel inhibited and insecure at first and less likely to play as a result. After a week or so you should start to see an improvement in your dog's attitude towards play while outside. You are now in a position to ask a friend, preferably one whom the dog knows, to put your dog's toy in their pocket and meet you out on a walk. As they approach, tell them not to look at or speak to the dog. After a few seconds of conversation instruct them to take out the toy and throw it down in front of the dog. You should encourage your dog to play with it for a few seconds before removing the toy and throwing it back to your friend. Tell them to hold it in a

visible position while you continue your conversation. Before you part company, tell them to throw the toy to the dog and you then have a good game with it.

The breakthrough comes when the dog starts to show signs of taking the thrown toy back to the other person in an attempt to continue the game, instead of playing with you. If the process is repeated over the next few weeks then you should end up with a dog that wags its tail when anyone approaches, in the anticipation of getting a game with the toy that just might be concealed in their pocket. Once this stage is reached you can then allow people to approach and offer the dog titbits or even to stroke it. When using titbits it is important to have several in each hand so that the dog is aware that both hands contain food. Always ensure that the last titbit left in one hand is never given to the dog. This ensures that the dog's focus of attention remains on the person's hands throughout. If the last titbit is given there is a danger that the dog's attention will move from the person's hands to his face and eyes, which may provoke aggression as soon as the last titbit has been eaten. I sincerely hope that this programme makes more sense to you than the system a great number of 'experts' advise of treating the problem by the use of aggression. Surely making your dog frightened of you is never the right way to make it less frightened of other people.

Chase aggression (predatory)

This problem is worse among the herding breeds such as Border Collies, Bearded Collies, etc. because it is an extension of the chasing instinct for which they have been bred. The chase aggressive dog does not begin its problems by being aggressive; that comes as a learnt experience much later, if at all.

When owners buy a young puppy that has a highly developed chasing instinct, the only game it will really want to play is the game of chase, usually with a ball that the owner has provided. During the games the pup is continually over-stimulated by the owner pretending to throw the ball one way, then turning and throwing the ball the other way. The pup will then race after the thrown toy and will either lose interest when the ball becomes stationary and it has circled the toy once, or will in fact pick it up and run around with it in its mouth. These games continue with the pup often learning to return with the toy and spitting it out as it approaches the owner, followed by a quick reversing act as it gets into a position of anticipation of the next chase for the ball. Owners will often kick the ball instead of picking it up and throwing it, thereby focusing the pup's attention on their feet as well as on the ball.

At no stage during the game will the owner instill any control whatsoever and so the growing puppy learns to become excited by rapid movements of either the ball or the owner's hands or feet. A large number of chase aggressive dogs live in households where there are children who add to the dog's chase education by racing back and forth, encouraging the pup to chase them. The game is made more exciting because when the pup starts to nip at their legs, they will simply take avoiding action the next time the game is played by anticipating the dog's likely action and trying to dodge it at the last second – all very exciting for the dog. This game obviously improves the pup's co-ordination, and it gets more and more skilful as the game progresses and will often invite the owners to play games of chase, even to the point of becoming a nuisance.

When the pup is taken out into the big wide world it will find a great deal more to excite its desire to chase, and top of the list will be people on bicycles, joggers, children and cars.

When the young dog gets excited and starts to set off on a game of chase, the owner cannot get the dog back, even if it is perfectly obedient at other times. The dog will race up to what it is chasing and usually, if the person stands still, the dog will circle round them once and then return to its owner quite happily. If the person tries to escape the dog will continue chasing. At this stage there is no aggression. Then comes the time when the dog engages in a chase and as it circles round the person at the end of the chase it is subjected to aggression by the person or child, who kicks out at it. You now have a chase aggressive dog who will chase anyone it sees moving rapidly and will run up behind them and nip their ankles before they can do anything about it. More usually it is children who are bitten by Border Collies and other chase-motivated dogs, as it would be unlikely that an elderly person would move fast enough to excite the dog.

The owner, of course, will punish the dog but the timing of the punishment is usually too late for the dog to associate it with its act of aggression. Nearly all dogs will associate the punishment with the fact that they have returned to their owner and the end result is a dog who gets better and better at its games of chase and worse at returning when called.

The programme for putting the owner back in control of a chasing or chase aggressive dog takes time and patience to carry out, but if done correctly will effect a complete cure.

Stage 1

Go out and buy a really exciting chasing toy such as a ball on a rope or a kong. (In case you are not familiar with a kong toy it is shaped in such a way that the bounce becomes unpredictable and it is therefore more exciting for a dog to chase [see illustration, page 37].) Remove all toys so that the dog cannot gain access to them. You are now going to re-educate your dog on chasing games.

If you own more than one dog you must split up the problem dog from other dogs (see nervous aggression). Pick any time that the dog gets excited in the house, produce your 'special' toy and tease the dog before throwing it. Allow the dog to chase and, if possible, retrieve the toy. Stop before the dog gets bored with the game. You must also stop your children running around and encouraging the dog to chase them. *All* chasing games are now played only with the toy.

Stage 2

You should now have a dog that is becoming obsessed with chasing the toy whenever it is produced, so you can now start teaching the chase recall.

Play with the toy three or four times each day for one week but before you commence the game, attach a length of washing line or similar to the dog's collar. Throw the toy a total of twenty times each day, but at random, twice out of the twenty times that it is thrown, you stop the dog when it is half-way between you and the toy by putting your foot on the line as you give the command to return, 'come' or 'here'. Insist that the dog comes all the way back to you by sharp jerks on the line. Praise well when it returns and go and pick up the toy yourself, fastening the line around something to prevent the dog from following. It is important that the dog is teased before throwing the toy and is not made to sit and wait. It is not an exercise that starts with control; it is a game for the dog. At the end of the week you should try the dog off the line to check its response. If it returns instantly when called when it is chasing the ball then go to Stage 4; if not – read on.

Stage 3

For one week increase the frequency of recalls to four in twenty at random and then try again off the line. If you still have difficulty then for a further week increase the frequency of recalls to six in twenty and so on each week until you reach a level where the dog still is keen to play the game but the game is under your control. If you overdo the number of times the dog is recalled then its desire to play will diminish.

Stage 4

Stop playing all games in the house with your dog and now take the toy out with you. It helps if you tease the dog with the toy several times before actually going outside. Find a quiet spot where there are no distractions and remove the lead, attaching a twenty-five-foot length of line to the collar in its place.

Now repeat your previous training by teasing your dog and then throwing the toy, allowing the line to trail. The frequency of recalls when your dog is between half and three-quarters of the way to the toy should be at the same level that enabled you to gain control when you played the game in your house. Remember that the dog must be taught to return instantly when called and to come all the way back to you, allowing you to recover the toy. Continue each day until you reach the stage where you can remove the line and still retain instant control over your dog.

Stage 5

Now go out to where there are going to be other people. For preference these should be people whom you know and who have been instructed to tempt the dog away from you. Attach the line and encourage your dog to run towards them, keeping your foot firmly on the end of the line. As the dog sets off, simply call it back in the same way as you have taught it to return when chasing a thrown toy. As the dog turns to come back, tease it with the toy and turn and throw it in the opposite direction, allowing him to chase and retrieve it (the line can be used to ensure that the dog brings it back to you.)

Repeat this daily until you are sure that you have total and instant control at a distance, at which point you should be fairly safe in removing the line.

With patience it is easily possible to teach a chase aggressive dog to become more interested in fulfilling its desire to chase by providing an outlet rather than trying to inhibit the dog's instincts. The many people that have successfully applied this programme to their dogs usually report after several weeks that the dog, when exercising free and at a distance, will instantly run back to the owner whenever a person runs or cycles past, anticipating a game with the toy.

The whole process of controlling chase games takes nothing but time, patience and a will to succeed. There are, of course, alternative methods based on making the act of chasing people unpleasant for the dog in question, but none of these can be used by the owner. These techniques can be applied only by the person being chased so the dog, by being subjected to a disagreeable experience, may not wish to repeat the activity that led to that experience.

Chasing after a dog that sets off to chase a person is by far the worst sort of action an owner can indulge in as the majority of dogs will believe that there is an element of competition over who is going to win that particular game and it will invariably teach the dog to run faster in order to beat the owner to the prize.

Avoidance learning techniques that can occasionally be applied successfully involve giving the dog a shock that in no way involves the use of physical force. These techniques would involve either giving the volunteer 'victim' something that makes a noise that will startle the approaching dog, such as a starting pistol, rape alarm or ultra-sound emitter, or using a high-powered water pistol. It is vital that the dog believes that the 'shock' has come from its victim and not the owner. The owner's role in these encounters should be inviting and rewarding, thereby making it a disagreeable experience if it sets off to chase anyone and a pleasant, rewarding alternative to remain close to its owner.

It is even more important that the owner uses games of chase with a toy to satisfy the dog's instincts.

Territorial aggression

This is the type of aggression where the dog will vigorously defend what it sees as territory belonging to it and not the owner. The smaller the territory the more aggression is shown, thus a territorially aggressive dog is usually worse in a car than in a large, open field.

For a dog to be territorially aggressive, then, it must see itself as the dominant one in the partnership between dog and owner. Is the dog dominant within the owner's house (excluding the garden)? If it is aggressive to the point of not allowing anyone in when the owner opens the front door then it must be either dominant with the owners, in which case applying the dominance programme should effect a cure, or nervous aggressive, in which case the nervous aggression programme should work.

A dog simply cannot be submissive towards its owner and territorially aggressive in the house, as the dog has no territory to defend – that's the role of the owner. There are, however, dogs that are submissive towards their owners within the house but territorially aggressive in the garden, exercise field or local park. That is, they will let anyone in the house and are always friendly but will threaten people who come into the garden, field, etc. To understand this more fully you simply need to substitute the word 'possessions' for 'territory'.

Take, for instance, a dog that is not allowed to win games, or possibly even play games, with toys in the house. It is, however, allowed to take its toys into the garden, and although it has played with its owners in that particular area, it has always won games of possession and retained the toys. We now have a dog that owns territory related to where it wins possession games in the confines of the garden, i.e. it is dominant in the territory of its garden but submissive when entering the territory of its owner's house. A large number of dogs that exhibit signs of territorial aggression will defend the area of territory that they see as belonging to them regardless of the point of entry into that area. This means that the dog will become aggressive when anyone tries to enter through the garden gate, although when the visitor enters the house the dog sees this as leaving *its* territory and entering the owner's domain. This explains why some dogs will let anyone into the house (the visitor is actually leaving the dog's territory and entering the owner's) but will attempt to bite them as they leave (the dog is trying to stop the visitor from entering its territory)!

The same thing applies to some dogs when exercised in the park. The dog will pick up a stick or the owner will throw a toy and the dog retains possession of the stick all the time it is in that area. Even though the owners can take toys away from the dog in the house, they find it difficult, if not impossible, to get toys or sticks away from the dog and keep them away while exercising in the park.

At the end of an exercise session the dog will give up the toy quite readily – as soon as it leaves the territory. We now have a situation where the dog is possessive, thus dominant, thus territorial in that area and will defend it against anyone it may see as an intruder.

Improving the dog's behaviour can be accomplished quite easily and quickly by following the guidelines below.

Remove all toys, chews, bones and other possessions from the garden. You can still play strength games but make sure you always win and retain possession of the toy. Never allow your dog to go into the garden unaccompanied for at least the next six weeks. Do not allow your dog to eat or take food into the garden and do not allow it to have any areas where it is allowed to curl up and go to sleep. If you accompany your dog each and every time it goes into the garden you will be on hand to administer verbal correction whenever it attempts to bark at anyone who goes past, and to reward him when he behaves correctly. This area will now slowly become your territory and not the dog's, thus removing the problem.

In the park, make sure to take a toy and make a point of playing with your dog several times during the walk, making sure that at the end of each short play session you retain possession of the toy and do not allow the dog to touch it again until you invite him to. Stop the game at random and put the toy away anywhere within that area; don't wait until you get outside the area. It also helps if you teach the dog to lie down instantly when it is told, thus reinforcing your dominance over your dog in that area.

There is also a case for being aggressive towards the dog yourself by shouting or forcing him to adopt the down position, or even striking him with your hand or shaking him by the scruff of the neck if he is a small dog. Remember, though, that in order to reinforce your dominance over the dog you have to be in the area with him at the time. It is useless to go into the garden and chastise your dog for biting the postman thirty seconds after the event. It has to be carried out instantly to be effective, so you must be in attendance in order to administer the correction.

Sexual aggression

This is almost as exclusively confined to male dogs who, although normally submissive, will mount or attempt to mount people and usually other dogs as well and will become increasingly aggressive if their victim tries to stop them from indulging in the act. Castration, sometimes combined with behaviour therapy, is the cure to the problem and is a matter for you to discuss with your vet.

Which type of aggression problem does my dog have?

That's the difficulty, because unless you know just why your dog is aggressive towards people or towards yourself then attempts to cure him will sometimes prove disastrous. We can summarise aggression towards people as follows.

Dominant aggression – usually only family members are initially threatened by a young dog. It is usually described as over-friendly to other people. Often referred to as Jekyll and Hyde in character or schizophrenic. Loves to be touched but usually on the dog's terms. Wins all games of possession, has exclusive sleeping areas – often bedrooms. Usually eats before the owners and often steals things that do not belong to it, hiding underneath or behind items of furniture when it needs to reinforce its position. As it matures, will often allow only certain people into its house and territory. Hates visitors going upstairs.

Nervous aggression – usually carbon copy of mum's behaviour, which is why 'breeders' (I use the term loosely) never let you see a nervous bitch with her puppies when you go to buy one. Aggressive behaviour is defensive in nature and so is always worse when the dog's escape route is cut off, i.e. when held on the lead or when visitors try to enter the house or room. Will usually be reasonably good in crowds but will be on edge when approached by a single person. Eye contact usually produces an aggressive reaction.

Territorial aggression – this takes place only if the dog is the dominant one in the partnership in that area, i.e. the dog and not the owner owns the territory. Any act on the owner's part to make the dog more submissive improves the dog's behaviour. Reducing the area that the dog perceives as its territory by exercising it in different areas on successive days, reducing territory marking (leg cocking in males) while on the lead and accompanying the dog on all excursions into the garden will rapidly improve the dog's behaviour.

Sexual aggression – the most appropriate cure for any animal who uses aggression to relieve sexual frustration is castration.

Car aggression problems directed towards people – dogs that behave aggressively in the car towards other people do so for most of the reasons mentioned above. Aggression towards owner characterised by any act on the owner's part, e.g. closing the door, changing gear, starting the engine, leads to displays of aggression by the dog. Treat as for dominant aggression.

Aggression towards people who come near when the owner is in the stationary car, but the dog is no problem when he is by himself in the car – treat as for nervous aggression.

Aggression towards people outside while the car is moving, typically with the dog flying at the windows – treat as for chase aggression by interrupting the dog's field of vision by the use of curtains or screens.

Aggression towards other people when the owner is not in the car and the dog is by itself. This is territorial aggression and the majority of the car-owning, dog-owning public would accept the dog's behaviour in this instance.

What the majority of car thieves do not realise is that if they opened the door the dog would be totally non-aggressive when outside the car!

It is important to point out once again that if you are experiencing any problems relating to aggression with your dog you should first consult your vet, who may then refer you to a recognised dog-behaviour consultant.

8

Dog/Dog Aggression

In general, dog-to-dog aggression problems are less easy to correct than the corresponding dog-to-human aggression problems. This is mainly due to the fact that in a dog-to-dog encounter you cannot use a cure such as getting the other dog to squirt water at your dog or throw a toy for it or feed it. It is therefore the owner who must always take the initiative in applying corrective measures, preferably in the first instance by using other dogs that are known, such as those in a training class.

As mentioned in Chapter 6, Owning More than One Dog, the majority of dog/dog aggression problems are learnt through early games. By allowing a young dog to play aggressive games with another dog to the point where the owner has no control over the games, you are sowing the seeds for dog aggression as your puppy starts to mature.

We will now examine each of the categories of dog/dog aggression in an attempt to understand how the problems are caused and the guidelines to use in modifying any aggressive behaviour.

Nervous aggression

There are three possible causes of nervous aggression towards other dogs. By far the most common problem is caused by a young puppy being attacked by another, older dog while out exercising. The pup does not need to be physically injured for this to occur; the mental shock of simply being bowled over is usually quite sufficient to leave the pup shocked and mentally scarred. If this happens only on one isolated occasion the resultant problem will often be breed-specific, which means that if the young dog was attacked by a black Labrador then it may never tolerate the presence of a black or chocolate Labrador again. Occasionally the problem may also be related to the area where the attack took place and so the dog will not accept any Labrador near it while exercising in the park but will be completely at ease if it encounters a Lab in the training class.

If the young dog is attacked or intimidated on several different occasions by different breeds of dogs, then the puppy may well become nervous and aggressive towards any other dog that comes near.

The second type of nervous aggression is caused by depriving a puppy of social contact with other dogs during the critical early period in its life, from four to sixteen weeks. This problem has increased over recent years since the onset of parvovirus. An average puppy owner will generally have been advised, by the breeder or vet, to avoid all contact with other dogs until the puppy has developed full immunity after a course of vaccinations.

When the pup is finally taken out in an attempt to socialise it with other dogs, the ageing puppy will usually feel frightened and intimidated by them and unable to cope with the situation. It then clings tightly to its owner in early encounters with other dogs, often not even daring to peek out to look from behind its owner's legs.

The aggressive side of its nervous nature starts to develop at around seven months of age when the owner decides to make an effort to 'socialise' it with other dogs in an attempt to improve its behaviour. It is often taken into a dog-training class where the whole experience of being thrust into such a hostile environment proves extremely frightening. Maybe other dogs are barking in the hall and the poor pup, having no visible means of escape, becomes extremely withdrawn and hides under its owner's chair.

It is usually around the third week of attendance that owners of young dogs that are nervous of other dogs start to notice a sudden, often dramatic change in their dog's behaviour. Now, whenever another dog approaches, the nervous pup starts to growl, turning its head away from the offending dog as it does so but still maintaining eye contact. By the fifth week of attendance, it only takes another dog to approach and our nervous young dog will fly out to snap at dogs and bitches alike. The aggressive phase of the nervous behaviour is now complete.

It should be pointed out that the dog could equally well be exposed to other dogs in the local park in an attempt to 'socialise' it and the end result will be the same; it is just accelerated by exposure to a large number of dogs in a closed environment.

The third major cause of nervous aggression towards other dogs comes about in an environment where a bitch that is herself nervous aggressive towards other dogs has a litter of puppies and they are brought up in an area where the bitch sees other dogs and is aggressive towards them in their presence. They then not only grow up to have learnt to be frightened of other dogs but will also have learned mum's aggressive techniques for regaining control of the situation. This is a learnt type of nervous aggression and need not be confined to exposure to a nervous mother. If a puppy is taken away from its litter-mates at between six and sixteen weeks and homed in an environment where there is another dog that is nervous towards other dogs, then the pup can easily pick it up from that dog. This is why it is so important to make sure that the dog you own has no behaviour problems related to nervousness before you purchase a young puppy.

Curing a dog that is nervous aggressive towards other dogs

In order actually to cure this type of problem the owner is faced with two difficulties, one being the availability of suitably good-tempered dogs to which to expose your nervous dog, and the second to get the dog to associate exposure to other dogs with a pleasant experience.

The three techniques I use almost exclusively are outlined below, and are usually adapted a) to suit the individual dog dependent on the extent of the problem, and b) to take into account the owner's resources in terms of volunteer dogs of known good temperament and their ability to motivate their nervous dog to play with a toy. The first method comprises four stages.

Stage 1

Find a toy that your dog really likes and remove all other toys. You must first work through the stages in motivating your dog to play with a toy as outlined in the cure for nervous aggression problems directed towards people (see page 120).

This should normally take between one and three weeks to get to the point where playing with you and the toy should be one of the highlights of your dog's day. Remember that if you own another dog, it must be separated for the duration of the programme. Separation means no sleeping together, playing together or any unsupervised access to one another.

Stage 2

Now stop playing all games with the dog in the house and take the toy outside when you exercise your dog. Go to a quiet area and encourage the dog to play. The more movement and excitement you can generate the better. You cannot command your dog to play with a toy! It helps if you tease the dog with the toy in the house before you go out. Even if your dog is unwilling to play initially when taken out for exercise, if you persist you will eventually get the dog to play quite enthusiastically.

Stage 3

Now when you go out, arrange to meet one or two dogs in a quiet area. Tease your dog with the toy before walking past each dog in turn at a distance of about ten feet. Try to keep your lead slack at all times. The lead is on no account to be used to jerk or correct your dog. Work hard to keep your dog's attention on the toy in your hand.

If you manage to get past successfully then you can have a good game with the toy before repeating the exercise. Suppose that your dog lunges out at the other dog. Well, the lead will prevent it from actually reaching the other dog and then, without pulling your dog back on the lead, try calling it away for a game with the toy. The owner of the other dog should remain stationary, keeping their dog under control. Persevere with this even if it takes a few minutes to get your dog to want to come to you to play with its toy. You will need to continue this process daily, using the same two or three volunteer dogs until your confidence builds. This would normally take two to three weeks.

Stage 4
Repeat Stage 3 but now release your dog from its lead and progressively decrease the distance between the two dogs as you pass. When you have passed the other dog successfully turn around and throw your toy in the general direction of the other dog and handler, encouraging your dog either to retrieve or play with it.

You may well find that when you get the passing distance down to four feet or so, your dog swaps over to walking on the opposite side, putting you between itself and the other dog. Do not prevent it from doing this.

After several such sessions your dog should have learnt to become excited at the approach of the other dog in anticipation of a game with its favourite tcy. Because of these pleasant associations surrounding contact with dogs that do not display aggression, your dog should quickly relax in the company of any strange dog of good temperament that you walk it past.

It is more than possible to get the dog to associate the presence of other dogs with a game so that every time that another dog comes into view, your dog looks up at you wagging its tail in anticipation of a game with its toy. If you then take your dog out and exercise it off the lead with two or, at the most, three other dogs and allow them to mix, occasionally calling your dog back to play with the toy, you should be well on the way to a total cure.

The only problem with using this method is that it is slow to produce results and most owners of problem dogs want a much quicker cure. I therefore sometimes use the second method initially until the owners have achieved success in Stage 3 of the previous programme, at which point the second method is reduced on a daily basis.

Before outlining this method it should be noted that it should not be used for puppies or growing young dogs, and it is vital that your dog is fit and in good health before commencing. Your vet should always be consulted before you even consider applying the following programme.

Stage 1
Make sure that clean, fresh water is always readily available throughout. Withhold all food for twenty-four hours. This

simply means that for most dogs that are on one meal per day you simply have to cut out feeding between meals. If there is normally food available ad lib throughout the day then for the duration of the programme you should allow your dog a maximum of only five minutes to eat its food before picking up its bowl and any remaining food in it. Continue feeding this way for one week and your dog should eagerly consume the contents of its bowl within the allowed time of five minutes.

Stage 2
When the next meal is due, mix up the food, tease your dog with it but do not allow it to eat. Divide the food into ten equal portions and enlist the help of two or three volunteers with other dogs.

Take your dog out on a lead with a carrier bag containing the ten portions of food placed in individual containers – plastic vending cups will do nicely. As you walk towards one of the dogs offer your dog the first container of food but with your hand held over the mouth of the container with your fingers apart, so that your dog can smell the food but cannot get it (see illustration). Walk past the other dog, passing at a distance of around ten to twelve feet, and providing the distraction of the food has been enough to prevent any aggressive reaction on your dog's part, allow him to eat the food in the container. If, on the other hand, your dog decides to look away from the food to bark/lunge or snap at the other dog, then remove your fingers

Correct finger placement when using food to overcome nervous problems

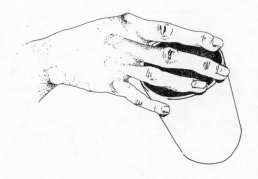

from the container and call the dog towards you. Do not jerk the lead or shout at your dog but try to use as much encouragement as possible to interest your dog in the food in your hand. If your dog comes away from the other dog within about five seconds, allow it to have one small mouthful of food from the container and then put the container of food away. If your dog is more interested in barking at the other dog, then this container is replaced in the bag. Repeat this only nine more times during this session.

Stage 3
Withhold all food until the next meal is due in twenty-four hours' time, and repeat Stage 2. What you will probably find is that the first day you do this your dog will eat only three containers and will therefore miss seven-tenths of his meal. This ensures that the following day he will be more likely to be distracted by the food than he is bothered by the presence of any of the dogs.

You can imagine that in two weeks' time, if the only food the dog is eating is when it approaches other dogs it will actually start to look forward to passing other dogs instead of fearing them. Because you cannot use this system for prolonged periods it is normally used only in conjunction with toys, with the toy game eventually replacing the food.

I cannot stress strongly enough that you should never use this method as a do-it-yourself cure but should apply it under guidance from your vet or the dog-behaviour consultant you are working with who will monitor the dog's progress closely to ensure that the programme is working correctly.

The third method, which is an avoidance learning technique, would again be applied in conjunction with either or both of the above methods, particularly in cases where there is a possibility of one of the volunteer dogs being bitten. First of all you need to have applied Stage 1 of method one or two. Then, when you take your dog out to meet your volunteers with their dogs, take out the toy or bag of food and then place your dog on a lead which is a minimum of six feet in length. Pre-arm your assistants with a washing-up-liquid container which has been carefully washed out and is filled with clean, cold water. They will also need a set of John Fisher's Dog Training Discs. Now as you approach the first dog with your toy or food inducement, hold on to the lead, keeping it quite short so that your dog feels some tension on his collar. Aim to pass the other dog at a distance of twenty feet. As soon as your dog lunges forward, immediately let go of the lead and turn and walk in the opposite direction, without saying a word. In most cases, when the dog realises that you are not trying to pull it back and have left it to its own devices it will turn away from the other dog and follow you. Reward it instantly if it does so.

If your dog continues to make its way towards the other dog(s) then the handlers should immediately squirt it with water and throw the discs while quickly walking *towards* your dog. As soon as your dog runs back to you, reward it. You must remember that you and the other handlers must not raise your voices; the shock of the cold jet of water hitting your dog and the clatter of the discs should do the trick. Reward your dog when it returns.

What your dog will learn in no uncertain terms is that:

a) his undesirable behaviour results in you walking away and leaving him on his own without your backing;

b) lungeing at other dogs does not result in them withdrawing or being pulled out of its way; in fact the opposite happens – they come towards him;

c) something unpleasant happens each and every time he is left out on a limb lungeing at other dogs. This unpleasant association is in no way connected with you but with the act of going for the other dogs.

If you put yourself in your dog's place you can see that in a very short space of time you would prefer the company of your owner rather than engaging in conflict with other dogs.

It should be noted that this, the third method in dealing with a dog that is nervous aggressive with other dogs, will not result in a dog that will become friendly with other dogs; it will simply learn to avoid them.

The best way of avoiding the possibility of ending up with a dog that is nervous aggressive with other dogs is to take your puppy along to one of the many good puppy-socialisation classes that are now being run, thanks largely to the influence of Mito Pearsall who pioneered puppy training back in the 1960s.

It is important to enrol in a class when your puppy is no more than sixteen weeks old.

Chase or predatory aggression

To understand chase-motivated aggression fully you should read Chapter 6, Owning More than One Dog, because that is where the vast majority of chase aggression problems are introduced.

The puppy first learns to chase and play fight with another dog on a regular basis, often reinforced by the unwitting owner who will chastise the older dog if it dares to growl or snap at the puppy during a play session. As the games progress, the pup merely improves his fighting skills and techniques and also his speed and co-ordination. This equips him perfectly for the fighting that he will engage in later in life when he encounters other dogs in his chase games.

The techniques used to modify the human version of our chase aggressive dog are used in dealing with inter-dog chase aggression. This involves the process of teaching the dog to do a chase recall exercise for a toy, which can then be used, if necessary, in conjunction with the food techniques described in the section on nervous aggression towards other dogs.

A professional training instructor will be able to teach you the technique necessary to regain control of your dog in this instance and it is more than possible to re-educate even confirmed chasers and fighters just by satisfying the dog's chasing instinct with a toy and then teaching a basic control exercise. Free running recalls on a thrown toy should then be practised on a daily basis. Remember to separate your dog if it normally lives with or has daily access to any other dog(s).

Dominant aggression towards other dogs

This is more often than not associated with male dogs, although the problem is not uncommon in bitches. Typically the dog will approach another dog of the same sex and rise up on tiptoe with the tail (if present) held high over the dog's back and wagging quickly from side to side. There is then a period of jockeying for position until the more dominant dog will push his head across the other dog's shoulders and will sometimes follow this up by placing one or both front paws on the other dog's shoulders, towering above it in the process.

What happens next is dependent on the behaviour of the other dog. If it shows signs of submitting then a fight is usually averted, but if it retaliates then there is often a fight where both dogs will throw themselves at one another and roll over and over as each one tries to gain the upper hand. There is always a tremendous amount of noise during these encounters, with most bites being confined to the head, neck and back regions.

This is the only aggression problem that can quite often be successfully dealt with by the owner taking the initiative and verbally and physically reprimanding their dog *before* the dog is engaged in a confrontation. This is best achieved by putting your dog in a submissive down position and insisting that he does not move. You will need either to attend your local dog-training club to learn how to teach this exercise, or read my previous book *Your Dog: Its Development, Behaviour and Training*, where the down exercise is explained in full.

The reason why lots of owners are unsuccessful in trying to punish their dogs physically for attempting to dominate other dogs is that their dog, in addition to being dominant with other dogs, is also dominant with them. Attempts to enforce control while the dog is behaving badly often result in the dog redirecting its aggression on to its owner. Many owners are bitten simply because they have tried to check their dog on the lead for growling at other dogs.

So in cases of dominant aggression problems with other dogs it is vital that the owner first applies the dominance programme to put them in control of their dog. Sometimes this alone is enough dramatically to reduce the dog's aggression towards others. If it isn't, then teaching the submissive down, first of all away from any distractions and finally in the presence of other dogs, will work. Once you have achieved this, you should then be in a position to control your dog totally in the presence of other dogs. Remember that if you apply correction *after* your dog has had an encounter with another dog it will be totally ineffective. It must be applied *before* any likely incident.

With male dogs that are dominant aggressive towards other male dogs, castration will often quickly improve matters, whereas spaying a bitch that is dominant is unlikely to effect an improvement and will sometimes make her worse.

The way I understand castration to work is that by reducing the level of testosterone, the dog ceases to be seen as much of a threat by other dogs in the neighbourhood and as such, is engaged in fewer dominant confrontations, whereas if you increase the level of testosterone then other dogs see this superstud as a major threat and so engage him in even more dominance confrontations.

If you are unwilling to take the step of having your dog castrated then speak to your vet about the possibility of hormone therapy as an alternative.

Territorial aggression

For territorial aggression towards other dogs, read the above section on Dominant aggression towards dogs (page 142) and the section on Territorial aggression (page 129) in Chapter 7, Dog/Human Aggression Problems.

Sexual aggression problems towards other dogs

The answer is the same as that given under the heading Sexual aggression (page 131). The belief some people hold is that if a dog is oversexed then presenting him with a bitch to mate will improve his behaviour. This is based entirely on myth. Allowing an oversexed and possibly aggressive dog to mate a bitch will always make its behaviour worse.

Summary of inter-dog aggression problems

Nervous aggression

Characterised by all or some of the following:

1. The dog usually displays aggression towards dogs and bitches alike, never taking the time to find out which is which before flying at them.
2. Behaviour is always worse when on the lead, cornered, in a confined space or in proximity to its owner.
3. In the early stages, the dog will often make a lot of growling/barking noises to warn away the offending dog before actually snapping at it.
4. The dog is often better when taken out by someone it does not know as it is unsure of anyone else's strengths and weaknesses in protecting it from the threat of other dogs.

Chase or predatory aggression

Characterised by all or some of the following:

1. The behaviour is usually worse when the dog is exercising off the lead.
2. The behaviour of the dog being chased will determine if there is to be an aggressive outcome.
3. The dog will return after nipping at the other dog and chasing it off the field.
4. The dog will often behave badly in the car when it is moving and it sees other dogs through the side windows.
5. Even if the dog is normally obedient and under control, once it has started to run towards another dog the owner is powerless to stop it.
6. The dog behaves exactly the same regardless of who takes it out for exercise.

Dominant aggression

1. More frequently seen in male dogs.
2. Often the dog is also dominant with its owners.
3. The initial approach is cautionary and often contains a number of status advertising rituals such as tail carriage, etc.
4. Fighting is always more severe than in chase or nervous aggression.

5. Behaviour is just as bad on or off the lead and whether or not the owner is present.
6. Frequent urination and scent-marking its territory.

Sexual aggression

1. Dog totally oblivious of its owner when it attempts to mount dogs and bitches alike.
2. Will often make squealing noises and 'high step' on the spot with its front legs.
3. Behaviour is the same both on and off the lead.
4. Bites are nearly always on the back of the other dog's neck or nose area and are delivered if the victim tries to avoid being manoeuvred into a position for mounting.

General

Most dog aggression problems have their roots in early games and contact with other older dogs. Controlling games that are played between dogs will usually give the owner control over each individual dog.

The worst combination of problems that you can possibly have is a dog that is both dominant and nervous aggressive. In cases such as these where there may be a multiple problem, you must always cure the dominance aspect first.

And finally, please be sensible about your attitude towards other dogs when you take yours out for exercise. Perhaps your dog is over-friendly with other dogs and you don't yourself have problems relating to aggression. Allowing your dog, particularly if it is a large one, to go bounding over to young dogs or puppies in the park could easily frighten an already nervous dog and will do nothing for its worried owner. If the other owner has aggression problems with their dog and yours goes bounding over, it's no use shouting 'It's all right, he's friendly' to the harassed owner who is trying hard to control a difficult dog.

If you are experiencing aggression problems with your dog, particularly those relating to nervousness, then do not allow other, loose dogs to approach and possibly intimidate it. This is particularly important where puppies are concerned. If you carry a water pistol with you it will put you in the position where you can prevent unwanted advances by other dogs, without in any way hurting them, just by squirting them with a jet of water. Your dog may well learn to rely on you when it is put under stress rather than to use its own teeth to defend itself.

9

Other Behaviour Problems

Destruction when left alone

To understand why dogs chew when their owners go out and leave them by themselves we need first to understand the mechanism by which they have learnt or rather been taught how to do it. So if you have a desire to teach your dog how to tear the house to pieces when it's left for even a few minutes, read on!

The process is usually started off with a young puppy by giving it a number of toys to play with and allowing them to be left lying around the house. The owners play with the new puppy frequently with these toys, particularly during the first month. So the pup learns that playing with toys, in itself a pleasant enough experience, is even better because it also gets the undivided attention of its owners during these games. After several weeks the pup will have started to use the toys to gain the attention of its owners, one of whom will always play when requested to do so by a little prompting with the toy.

The pup now starts to make more and more demands for attention by using its toys, and the owners rapidly reach a point where they tire of playing so many games on the pup's insistence. They now start to reject the pup's constant demands to play and so the pup goes from person to person, inviting them to play with a toy. No one is interested and so it possibly tries again with a different toy. Still no one is interested. The pup wanders off, still in a playful mood and wanting some attention. It then playfully puts its teeth on the leg of the coffee table or starts to pull a few strands of thread in the carpet and the owners quickly respond by telling it that it mustn't use its teeth on the furnishings but only on a toy, which they then give it and encourage it to play with.

Can you see what the pup is being taught? If no one will give it the attention it requires then playfully biting an item of furniture will prompt the owners to interact by offering it a toy. It will then alter its behaviour slightly to ensure that the owner is taking notice. This is how it happens. The very first time that biting the furniture produced the desired response it happened by accident rather than by design, the pup being unaware that the owner would respond by going over to him.

After two or three repetitions, when the pup deliberately wants to gain attention, it will go over to an item of furniture and turn round to watch for the owner's reaction as it starts to put its teeth on to chew it. This is as if to say, 'Excuse me, but have you noticed that I want some attention?' The owner, of course, immediately complies with the pup's wishes, even though, in human terms, the attention it starts to receive my involve a small measure of shouting or even attempts to smack it. These are usually only threats, but even if the owner actually smacks the dog this will happen so long after the event that it would be extremely doubtful if the dog could ever link the punishment with the crime it has committed.

We now have a situation where in order to gain attention the pup has learnt to put its teeth on various items of furniture. If the owners want to leave the pup in the house by itself they will normally gather up one or two toys to leave for the pup to play with while they are out. The pup now gets excited at the prospect of playing a game and, lo and behold, it suddenly finds itself all alone with no one to play with. What do you have to do to get your owners to return and give you some attention? That's it, chew the leg of the coffee table. After five minutes of chewing, with its eyes fixed firmly on the door its owners went out of, it decides that chewing the coffee-table leg has not had the desired effect and so turns its attentions to the carpet, which it understands usually works slightly better. When that, too, fails it progresses to the cushions, understanding that it nearly always produces the desired reward of attention.

And so it continues to experiment, moving from one thing to another until, at last, the owner returns to give it some attention. And what is the first thing every owner does as soon as they walk through the door and see the pup has been chewing? They take the pup over to what it has chewed and advertise the fact that it was the chewing that has brought them back to the house!

This time any punishment that is meted out to the pup is certainly never going to be associated with the act of chewing. Most dogs simply learn that when the owner returns home and utters the words 'Who's done this', it is about to be punished. Some clever dogs may learn to associate the fact that the cushions are off the three-piece suite with the owner's anger, but would never realise that it was their *act* of pulling off the cushions some time earlier that caused the punishment.

So you can easily end up with a dog that looks guilty and runs away and hides when the owner comes in and the cushions are on the floor and yet is happy to greet them when they come home and the cushions are not on the floor. How the cushions came to get on the floor in the first place would never be part of the association in the dog's mind.

Thus some owners know that the dog has been chewing as soon as they walk in the door to find it hiding in the corner looking worried, whereas if they return home when nothing has been touched, the dog greets them happily. It's the same simple association of chewed carpet equals punishment, irrespective of *who* chewed the carpet. Untouched carpet equals *no* punishment. Remember that the pup, in its own eyes, has never been punished for chewing the carpet; it's been punished for being in the same room as the chewed-up carpet, and there is a world of difference between the two. With this type of chewing for attention, it nearly always has the desired effect of teaching its owners to leave it less and less and for shorter and shorter periods.

It is also never only one thing that has been chewed but lots of things, frequently mass destruction of every conceivable item. After an absence of only thirty minutes the owner comes home to find the carpet shredded, the vinyl floor ripped, the door frame chewed, the three-piece suite torn apart, the curtains down and wallpaper removed from the wall.

The problem is made worse if the dog is allowed to have access to the owner twenty-four hours each day by allowing it to sleep in the bedroom. This means that, although the dog may well separate itself from its owner for short periods each day to relax, the doors to each room are always left open to allow the dog to make contact whenever it wishes. In extreme cases the owner cannot even go to the bathroom and close the door without the dog objecting and wanting to follow.

Most owners believe that they have a problem only when they go out of the house. This is rarely the case because with most destructive dogs they would behave in the same way if the owner put them in another room to where they are, closed the door and ignored them for an hour.

So the first part of the cure does not involve going out and leaving the dog; it involves teaching it to spend short periods by itself each day. Do not apply this to young puppies that are going through the teething process or to a dog that occasionally chews one or two carefully selected items.

Stage 1

For one week, wind down the attention that you give your dog on his demands. If he comes over and puts his nose under your hand, tries to climb on your knee, makes whining noises or scratches your leg with his paw to gain attention, then turn away and ignore him. Ignoring means you must not look at the dog, touch him or speak to him if he is the one making the demands. This, of course, does not mean that you have to ignore him all the time, only when he demands attention.

Stage 2

For a further seven days, teach your dog to spend five minutes by itself, confined to a room next to where you are sitting. This should ideally be carried out three times each day in the following manner.

Place things that will make a noise if they are disturbed, such as lemonade tins with a marble inside, against or on top of anything that is likely to be touched. Then put a chair with a metal tray fixed to the back just inside the door of the room in which the dog is going to be left. Put the dog in this room quietly without exciting it and close the door. You should now sit close to the door and time five minutes on your watch. You will probably hear your dog sniffing at the bottom of the door, followed by whimpering, and that is usually followed by the dog disturbing one of your strategically placed audible chewing indicators (lemonade tins). As soon as you hear this noise, flick open the door just far enough to throw a check chain, bunch of

Tea tray placed on chair back ready to be used for 'shock' treatment to prevent barking or chewing when left

keys or anything that will make a noise through the door to strike against the tray. Do not aim at the dog. Close the door instantly. The whole process of opening the door, throwing the keys and closing the door should ideally take less than two seconds.

Do not shout or otherwise advertise your presence to the dog when you carry out this 'correction' as we do not want to link its association with the shock in any way with you.

Reset your watch again for five minutes and repeat, and reset the five minutes each time you have to throw something at the tray. Do not enter the room until the dog has managed to remain in the room, without disturbing anything, for the whole duration of time on your watch. When you achieve this first complete five minutes, go into the room with a toy and have a good game with your dog. Repeat this process three times every day. It is always the first day that is the worst, so be patient if the first time you try this it takes more than an hour to get the full five minutes.

In one week's time, or when you have reached the point where on three successive days you have achieved a full five minutes without having to correct your dog, you can move on to Stage 3.

Stage 3
Now start increasing the time the dog is left in the room by itself by five minutes every day until you reach a maximum of thirty minutes. You can now reduce the number of times you perform

this each day down to just once. When you manage three successive days without problems you can move to Stage 3.

Stage 4

If your dog is used to sleeping in the bedroom, this is an excellent opportunity to move his bed outside the bedroom door. Set up the chair and tray just before you go to bed and close the door to maintain the association that you have started. Keep a bunch of keys handy just in case of problems. You should also repeat Stage 2 using a few different rooms if possible to accustom your dog to be by itself in any room you choose to put it into.

Stage 5

With the majority of dogs you can miss out this stage altogether. It is necessary to implement it only if your dog is all right when you are in the house, sitting in the next room, but is destructive when you actually leave the house. In other words, the dog differentiates between when the owners are in the house and when they have gone out.

You will first of all have to make a note of all the things you normally do before leaving the house. That would normally involve a set routine of brushing your hair, putting your keys in your pocket, putting on your coat, putting the dog in the kitchen and then going out.

Now you will need to go through the ritual of performing the whole of your going-out routine before leaving your dog in one of the rooms you have trained it to stay in. Then go and open the front door and close it again but don't actually go out. Instead, creep back into the room alongside where your dog is, using the shock treatment if and when you hear any disturbance.

You are now teaching your dog to disregard all the signals you give when you are going out and it puts you in the position where you are on hand to administer correction.

Stage 6

You can now go out of the house for increasing periods of time starting at fifteen minutes, but before going out put the chair and the tray by the door just to maintain the association. When you close the door in the room where you have left your dog, place a recently worn item of your clothing just *OUTSIDE* the door, on the floor. It also helps if you leave either the radio or television switched on, or in extreme cases you could record a normal half-hour conversation between family members and everyday sounds of the house when there are people in and play this tape every time you go out during this stage.

Now your dog will:

a) believe that you are sitting just the other side of the door, because most dogs sniff the bottom of the door to establish if the owner is present. It will, of course, smell the item of clothing you have left. You cannot leave the clothing in the room with the dog because the dog will see that it is not you;

b) have learnt that by relaxing without disturbing anything you will return and reward it by playing with a toy;

c) understand that if it tries to chew or disturb anything *the door* will get aggressive! The door, of course, will always be there.

Other things that help the dog to accept being by itself are:

1. Reduce the amount of contact that you have with the dog for thirty minutes before you leave it, so that the difference between you being present and being absent is much less noticeable to the dog.

2. You must ensure that you make a particular effort to leave the dog by itself for several short periods at weekends otherwise if it has a lot of attention on Saturday and Sunday it will object to being left by itself on Monday. The worst day of the week for problems of destruction is Monday in a normal week or Tuesday after a Bank Holiday!

You should also get into the habit of closing doors behind you so that the dog is not allowed to follow you everywhere you go in the house.

There is a second, more dramatic method which works extremely well but must be used with extreme caution. It should never be used on dogs that are frightened of thunder or gunfire and should never be used on puppies. You simply go through all the stages mentioned earlier but omit the chair and the tray.

You obtain a few devices known as 'exploding detonators'

and place them underneath anything the dog is likely to disturb or chew. When it does so the device is triggered and makes a loud bang. Dogs usually associate the act of chewing with the disagreeable experience very quickly and it is possible, using these devices, to correct even an older confirmed chewer in a very short space of time. This is to be used only as a last resort and under the guidance of a vet or behaviour consultant. Again it does not link the shock with the owner but with what it was doing at the time – chewing.

The final, ultimate solution is to buy a wire mesh cage, crate or indoor kennel into which the dog can be placed for short periods whenever it is left, physically preventing it from chewing. The dog must, of course, be conditioned to use the cage by feeding it in there every day for a week or so and putting it in while you are sitting watching the television, etc. Going into the cage should never be viewed by the dog as any form of punishment.

There are other reasons that dogs chew when they are left which are much easier to deal with, such as insecurity, which is characterised by the dog selectively chewing something that smells of the owner like a recently handled item or small piece of recently worn clothing. To counteract this you can either leave an old cardigan or pullover in with the dog for it to lie on when you go out or alternatively allow it access to your bedroom, the

Wire mesh indoor kennel

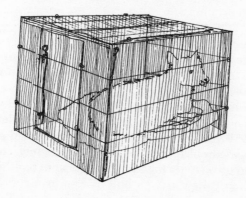

area in the house smelling strongest of you and to your dog, the most secure.

The other problem of chewing out of boredom is usually an indication that the dog is not being given enough physical or mental exercise. Increasing the games you play and the amount of physical activity during the time you are available should improve things. Also leaving a large hide chew for the dog to amuse itself with only when it is to be left for short periods will give it something to occupy its mind. Make sure that the chew bone is taken away from the dog when you come home otherwise your dog will chew it continuously and therefore be less likely to amuse itself with the bone when you go out.

It is also important to ensure that, if you catch your dog in the act of chewing, you should not shout at it or attempt to chase and smack it. Instead try throwing something soft and heavy at him so that he gets a shock associated with what he was doing at the time.

Barking

The environmental nuisance created by dogs that bark probably results in more complaints than any other nuisance associated with dog ownership. We shall start by examining one of the most common forms of barking and one of the easiest to cure – barking for attention when left. For a dog to learn to bark for attention, the young puppy's behaviour closely follows the behaviour of the pup that learns to chew to gain attention.

Quite often on the very first night it spends with its new owners the pup barks and howls through the night and is immediately rewarded for his behaviour by the owner returning to him. Within a couple of nights the pup is either taken up to the bedroom or the owner sleeps downstairs with it. If it is then inadvertently shut in a room by itself the resulting barks will rapidly bring the owner along to open the offending door.

Because barking that starts within five minutes of the owner going out is directed at the door through which they left, it is possible to use exactly the same treatment as for chewing when left, only omitting the chair and tray and substituting a water pistol squirted at the dog through the smallest opening possible. Just remember that you must not advertise the fact that it is you who is applying the shock; you want your dog to believe that it is the door applying the shock.

An alternative would be to use a blast from an aerosol rape alarm, or the chair and tea-tray method, but I would imagine that your neighbours will stop complaining about the dogs barking and start complaining about the noise you are now making!

Barking out of excitement

This type of barking is generally the forerunner to a really exciting event such as going out for a walk, being let off the lead to exercise or getting into or out of the car. It is characterised by being much higher in tone and continuous, subsiding only when the initial burst of excitement has died away.

A regime of subjecting the dog to frequent exposure to all of the preliminary events leading up to the anticipated reward is usually effective. It works like this. The owner puts on his coat and picks up the dog's lead; the dog, recognising that this means it is going out for a walk, starts to charge towards the door barking hysterically in anticipation of the exercise session. Once the dog has been placed on the lead and is outside the house the excitement starts to subside.

So to eliminate the problem simply go through the normal going-out ritual of putting on your coat, walking to the door, etc. then pause and count to ten. Now turn away from the door, take off your coat, hang the dog's lead back up and sit back down again. If you repeat this routine as often as you can, going out for a walk only about once in ten visits to the door, and even then only when all barking/excitement has ceased, you will with patience and perseverance cure the problem. When applying this technique it is important that you remain calm and quiet throughout.

Shouting will result only in the dog barking louder to make itself heard over the top of your voice. If you think about it, if you get excited and start shouting then your dog will not see your behaviour as being any different from its own.

The second way of dealing with the problem is by using an atomised spray of taste deterrent such as Bitter Apple into the air in front of the dog so that opening its mouth to bark produces an unpleasant taste. If using a proprietary taste deterrent, always follow the manufacturer's instructions for use. Dog training discs can also be of great benefit and come with a complete set of instructions.

Territorial barking

Although not strictly a problem, this is the type of barking where the dog hears a noise and starts barking to alert the family and to warn off the prospective intruder. This is, of course, welcomed by the majority of dog owners but can easily become a problem when the dog becomes over-enthusiastic and continues to bark even when the person walking by has long since passed and the owner continually shouts at the dog to be quiet.

Most dogs when hearing someone approach with whom they are not familiar will bark a number of times and then stop to listen in order to establish whether the person is still approaching or retreating. If the person is apparently getting closer, the barks, although around the same in number, will get louder. If, on the other hand, the person is now moving away from the house, the barks continuously diminish in both number and volume. Thus my Giant Schnauzer will bark three times with a half-second interval between barks immediately followed by two very quick barks. This sequence of five barks is followed by two to three seconds of silence after which the barking will either recommence with the same sequence, getting louder, or will start to decline, with the omission of the final two rapid barks and longer gaps between barks.

To enable the owner to be able to control the number of times that the dog barks to warn of impending danger, we must clearly teach the dog to understand and obey the command of 'quiet' at the time when the dog is most receptive to actually hearing it. So you must first learn your dog's barking sequence by counting the number of barks so that you can anticipate the second or two of silence in which you will have to introduce your command.

You will need the services of a friend to walk past the house two or three times each day for two to four days while you are training your dog. They should be instructed to walk past until they hear the dog start to bark, whereupon they should stand still for a minute or so before continuing on their way, standing still again if the dog begins barking once more. You should arm yourself with the dog's favourite toy or favourite food treat and wait until the barking starts.

Count the number of barks and anticipate when the dog will momentarily pause. If you then immediately give your command of 'quiet' and reinforce it with either a game with the toy or offering the food while continuing with a great deal of verbal and physical praise the barking should cease for a minute or so because the person outside is stationary and the dog is being distracted by your reward. The barking may possibly start again when your assistant moves off outside but simply keep repeating your sequence of silence, command then reward as much as is necessary. After several repetitions over two days you can now give your command of 'quiet' at the appropriate moment but now start to delay the reward so that the dog has to remain silent for two seconds before the reward is offered, then three, then four, then six and so on. If the dog barks, simply repeat the command and make it wait a few seconds more before rewarding it. When you can successfully give the command 'quiet' and reward the dog some twenty seconds or so later you can dispense with the services of your friend and then use this technique each and every time the dog barks when it hears someone or something. Vary the point at which the reward is offered after the command 'quiet' is given between three and thirty seconds, thus making it more unpredictable and thereby maintaining the dog's attention.

This technique relies on rewarding the periods of silence rather than punishing the barking and is extremely effective in putting the owner in complete control while not diminishing the dog's desire to give warning of an intruder.

The system of administering verbal punishment for barking usually serves only to compound the problem as the dog will frequently believe that its owner is in fact barking at the threat in competition with it!

Food stealing

Food stealing by itself is not a serious problem and can be avoided by ensuring that all food is kept out of reach of the dog, but some dogs are particularly adept at finding ways of opening cupboard doors, climbing on to work surfaces, etc., making the elimination of the problem unavoidable if the relationship between dog and owner has started to deteriorate. The more serious problem of aggression over food is made considerably worse if the dog takes to stealing food belonging to its owner and subsequently guarding it. As with all other behaviour problems it is essential to establish that the problem does not have its cause in the dog's overall health. A check-up by your vet will eliminate obvious physical reasons for the dog's desire to steal food and should always be the first course of action in dealing with the problem.

If the problem relates to a puppy or to a dog that is not fully mature, then by using a taste deterrent such as Bitter Apple on a few selected items of food strategically placed where food is usually available will be enough to prevent the problem developing any further.

For an adult dog that has learnt to steal food when the owner is not in attendance (most dogs learn that if they attempt to steal food when the owner is present, the owner becomes aggressive), a system has to be used whereby the dog learns that the act of stealing produces a disagreeable experience which is not connected in any way with the owner. This is known as environmental correction and is dealt with more fully in Chapter 10, You, the Owner.

Basically it involves using a small item known as a detonator placed under food or inside cupboard or fridge doors. The device uses a small percussion charge which is triggered by the movement of whatever is placed upon a spring mechanism. Once set, the device is positioned under food or inside a door and as soon as it is disturbed will make a loud bang which is usually sufficient to startle the dog. Two or three repetitions are usually required to drive the message home and permanently cure the problem, provided it is used under expert guidance.

Because of the obvious danger of abuse, this method is best

used only when taste deterrents and other means have failed, and then only on fit, healthy, adult dogs that do not have noise-associated fear problems. The detonators themselves are completely safe and cannot physically harm a dog but could cause stress-related problems if used inappropriately on the wrong type of dog.

A water pistol squirted at the dog every time it goes near food is a safe alternative and providing you do not shout and advertise the fact that it is you who is the cause of the sudden shock, the dog should associate the act of stealing with a disagreeable experience which is unconnected with your presence. You can then go out of the room and watch through a gap in the door, repeating the 'shock' of squirting water if necessary. This system also works extremely well with cats.

Food aggression

For minor food aggression problems such as growling, where the dog has not made any attempts to snap or bite, using the method described in Chapter 3, Surviving the First Six Months (pages 62–3), should cure the problem. For dogs where the aggression problem is more serious, the following steps must be used in conjunction with the method described.

Stage 1
First switch to a really bland-tasting type of food. There is evidence to suggest that some of the highly palatable tinned foods are so tasty that they are more likely to provoke severe aggression where the dog is already predisposed to the problem. Sometimes simply by changing to a nutritious but less appetising food the dog becomes uninterested in guarding its food. This, of course, needs to be carried out in conjunction with your vet who will have a lot of knowledge of remedial diets.

Stage 2
If, after both changing the dog's diet and carrying out the sequence described earlier, you cannot see a distinct improvement after two weeks then start feeding your dog in an area of territory away from its usual feeding place (often the kitchen) such as the garden or garage and substitute its food bowl for a

flat plate. It is often the case that it is either the area of floor or the bowl itself that is being guarded. For this reason you would normally notice much more severe forms of aggression if the dog's food bowl is left near to its bed in the kitchen. Continue feeding this way for a further two weeks, using a lead for control in order to move the dog gently away from its food, and titbits to reward the correct behaviour. If you still fail to see an improvement then go to Stage 3.

Stage 3
Raise the height at which the dog's food plate is placed to prevent the dog standing directly over it. The correct height should be such that with all four feet on the ground, the plate is level with the top of the dog's shoulders. It is now a very simple process to put the previous stages into effect to produce the desired result.

It is important that you do not show aggression by shouting or attempting to smack your dog for guarding its food as this will immediately make your dog see you as even more of a threat, thereby increasing its aggression towards you.

Remember that it is fairly easy to correct food aggression in a puppy but the problem usually gets more and more difficult to correct the longer it is left. Dogs seldom grow out of this type of behaviour; it invariably gets worse as the dog grows older.

Housetraining problems

We can divide housetraining problems into four basic areas.

1. Unclean at night when owners go to bed.
2. Unclean when owners go out but all right at night.
3. Will foul after returning from exercise.
4. Territorial marking (male dogs).

Dealing with each problem in turn we can see that the problem of the dog being unclean at night is characterised by the dog relieving itself on the floor, usually near a door, particularly if the dog is kept in the kitchen overnight. It is not a coincidence that this is usually the spot where the owners left newspaper down during the first few weeks of housetraining. So the problem has simply become a habit where the dog wakes up some time shortly before its owners and feels the need to relieve itself. It moves away from its bed and sniffs around to locate the correct spot and then relieves itself, returns to bed and settles back down to sleep.

To cure the problem it is simply a matter of restricting the dog in such a manner that it is impossible for it to move away from its bed. This is simply done by making use of an indoor kennel into which the dog is placed at night for a week or so. The kennel itself needs to be large enough for the dog to turn around and stretch but no more.

Accompany your dog on its last exercise session before you retire for the night so that you are in a position to reward it when it relieves itself. It is extremely important that the dog does actually relieve itself before it is placed in the kennel. Put it in the kennel and close the door. Leave all the doors open between the room where your dog is and your bedroom, or use a baby alarm. This is so that if your dog makes a noise in the night to attract your attention, you will be better able to hear and take it out to relieve itself.

What usually happens is that when the dog wakes up in the early hours of the morning and realises it cannot get to the desired spot that it sees as its toilet area, it simply turns round and goes back to sleep. As soon as you get up in the morning you must go and take your dog out for exercise, rewarding it when it 'performs'.

While you are retraining your dog you will have to remove all traces of smell on the floor by treating it with a biological washing powder in a solution of water, applied on a daily basis. This is so that when you allow your dog its freedom from the kennel, all trace of smell has disappeared, preventing the habit from re-forming.

The second of our housetraining problems, namely unclean when left by itself when the owners go out but generally all right during the night, is fairly typical of a dog that is suffering from separation anxiety. The reason the dog is usually clean through the night is due to the fact that it sleeps in, or has access to, the bedrooms. Because this dog has never learnt to be separated from its owner, when it is put in this position it becomes stressed with the resultant bladder and bowel control problem.

The attention the dog receives from its owners when they return home usually compounds the problem in one of two ways. First, if the owner is physically aggressive towards the dog on returning home the dog is placed under even more stress on subsequent occasions, and second, the attention the dog receives for its misdemeanours may well be preferred to the other extreme of no attention at all. Quite often the owners then return home to find not one large pile of faeces but lots of small piles, in the same way that a dog that chews to gain attention will rarely chew just one item but several different articles.

The cure for this type of problem is approached in the same way that you would treat a dog that chews to gain the attention of its owner.

Stage 1
An indoor kennel is a must in order to correct this type of problem. Start by putting your dog into the kennel for a period of five minutes twice a day for the first week. Stay in the room with the dog while it is in the kennel but do not speak to it or look at it, even if it makes a noise to gain attention. All you are trying to do initially is to teach the dog to accept being physically parted from you for a few minutes while you are there.

Stage 2
In one week's time, particularly if your dog sleeps in the bedroom, use the kennel at night to prevent it gaining access to you and to continue the process of getting it used to the kennel for increasing lengths of time.

Stage 3
One week after starting Stage 2, move your dog out of the bedroom by moving the kennel closer and closer to the door, eventually moving it outside the bedrooms altogether. You may need to leave the bedroom door open for a few nights so that the dog can still see you, and then start closing it by degrees until the dog accepts being by itself at night. When this stage is reached you can go on to the final stage.

Stage 4

Try going out for short periods of up to but not exceeding one hour, placing your dog in its kennel before you do so. Decrease the amount of contact that you have with him for twenty minutes or so before you go out. When you return, take the time to have a game with a toy and praise well. After one week you should be in a position to go out for longer but leaving the cage door open and allowing your dog access to all of the downstairs rooms. If, in the unlikely event of returning home you find that your dog has relieved itself on the floor, simply ignore the fact and praise and fuss it regardless. Remember to use a biological washing powder to clean up later and you should find that the problem disappears. You could, of course, continue to use the indoor kennel for increasing periods of time but I personally am not in favour of keeping a dog confined in this way while the owner goes out for several hours at a time.

For the dog that relieves itself on the carpet or doormat as soon as it returns from exercise, the solution is very simple. After giving your dog ample time and opportunity to relieve itself while exercising (and that means energetic running exercise and not simply a slow walk around the block), return home. If it did not relieve itself during the exercise session restrict it to its bed by making it physically impossible for it to get off its bed. This can be accomplished by fastening the dog on to a lead with a good swivel clip or a benching chain and fastening the lead or benching chain to the dog's bed, or by putting it into an indoor kennel, thus denying it access to the areas where it is likely to foul.

Wait for about twenty minutes or so and then take the dog back out. You should find that your dog will quickly relieve itself, when you should praise it well. When you return home you can allow your dog its freedom until the next exercise session is due. If the dog did not relieve itself, then repeat the above. If this is repeated each and every time the dog is taken out you will completely break the habit by making it impossible for the dog to relieve itself anywhere but in the correct place.

For all housetraining problems the type of food given to the dog can have some bearing. Some types of food, notably certain dried complete meals, result in the dog passing a large proportion of what they have eaten, which results in the requirement to pass motions much more frequently than dogs fed on a more digestible diet. It stands to reason that a dog that needs to relieve itself only three times in every twenty-four hours is going to be much easier to housetrain than a dog that needs to go six times or more.

Urine marking in male dogs

Some male dogs urinate against furniture, etc. without the owners being aware of it until they lift a carpet and find that it is wet through or until they come to move an item of furniture. This is because the dog will rarely if ever do it in view of the owners. It is always more pronounced in situations where there are other dogs visiting the household regularly or where more than one dog is owned.

A survey carried out by one of my colleagues, Hazel Palmer, suggests that in the majority of cases of urination in the home surgical castration will greatly improve the situation. I had previously used several methods of curing this problem with varying degrees of success but now rely on castration above all others as a cure.

Coprophagia (faeces eating)

This habit is varied in form and may simply consist of the common desire to eat horse, cow, sheep and rabbit droppings which, although perfectly natural to the dog, owners find disgusting to say the least. It is quite often seen in 'town dogs' that do not have regular access to farmland and these novelty foodstuffs! If you want to stop your dog from eating the dung of other animals then you will have to set up a suitable ambush in the form of a sudden shock such as a set of dog discs thrown at the dog or a water pistol squirted at it each and every time it goes near droppings. This correction should be environmental in nature rather than coming from the owner otherwise it will work only when the dog is in range of its owner's aim.

The problem of a dog eating its own faeces occurs in the first instance often as a result of feeding dried complete meals, a quantity of which passes through undigested. The dog is therefore encouraged to eat this undigested material and the habit starts up to the extent that in some cases even by altering the dog's diet the problem remains.

The addition of a small quantity of canned pineapple to the dog's diet usually effects a cure by making what comes out at the other end completely unpalatable to the dog. Iron tablets prescribed under veterinary supervision are a useful alternative in breaking the habit.

Unfortunately some dogs progress to eating the faeces of other dogs, which is a great deal more difficult to cure. The solution is to go out and spray all visible dung with a proprietary taste deterrent before exercising the dog. Splitting its meals into three and feeding each small meal before exercise will also reduce the dog's desire to eat anything further while exercising.

The problem could also be a medical one, which is why it is important that you consult your vet in the first instance.

Car travel

Car-travel problems can be notoriously difficult to deal with, particularly if the problem is one of long standing. As with all problem behaviour, before any treatment can be applied the cause has first to be established, so we will now take a look at the more common car-travel problems with a view to understanding and curing them.

Barking and associated attention seeking while the car is in motion

This problem is such that the dog's barking is almost continuous throughout the journey and is directed at its owner(s) who are sitting in the front seats. More often than not this type of dog has a great deal of access to its owner during the day and often during the night as well.

The problem starts because the dog wants to position itself in front of its owner to maintain facial contact in the way that it does in the house. For the first time in its life it is placed in the position where it is forced to look at the back of its owner's head. Frustrated by the lack of attention it receives, it starts to whine and then bark. The owner immediately turns round to tell the dog to be quiet, thereby satisfying the dog's desire for the owner to turn round and look at it. The more the owner turns to shout at the dog, the more the dog's behaviour is reinforced and rewarded.

The mounting anger in the owner's voice becomes merely an empty threat, particularly as the dog is behind a dog guard or in a cage and knows that its owner cannot get at it. The end result of the owner's shouts is that the dog barks with renewed vigour and barks louder and louder to make itself heard above the noise made by its owner.

To cure the problem you must remove the reward that the dog receives for its undesirable behaviour.

If you own a cage that fits inside the rear of your car, the process is made easier by removing it and placing it in your living room behind the position in which you normally sit. This will enable you to teach your dog to accept being put in a position where it cannot see your face, and you are now well placed to correct your dog when it starts to bark for attention. The whole process is therefore shortened because you will be able to train your dog more times in a week than by using the car alone.

The technique is to place the dog either behind the guard in

Purpose built dog cage fitted behind rear seats ensures the comfort and safety of both dog and driver

the car or in the cage in your living room and quietly sit in the front seat or chair. If you are in the car, do not start the engine. As soon as your dog starts to bark, without turning round to look and without saying a word create a small shock by either throwing a check chain over your shoulder to rattle against the cage (there should be no danger of the chain actually striking the dog) or using taste deterrent spray over your shoulder in the direction of your dog. Keep repeating this until you manage to get two full minutes of silence and then turn round and give your dog a lot of verbal praise. Repeat as often as possible, each day slowly increasing the length of time the dog is required to remain silent. When you can get fifteen minutes of silence for three consecutive days without having to apply the 'shock' treatment, you can simply take a passenger for a short ride in your car, instructing them to apply the shock as necessary while you are driving.

Your dog should quickly learn that barking, far from gaining attention, now results in a disagreeable experience, whereas silence produces the reward of being spoken to (it's not a good idea to turn round while you are driving but it is acceptable for the passenger occasionally to turn and reward the dog for its silence).

Fear of car travel

Fear of both the sound and, more important, the movement of the car frequently occurs in a young dog to the point where it becomes increasingly difficult actually to get the dog inside the car. In a short space of time the dog not only becomes frightened of the car itself but will often start to show signs of fear when it is taken out for a walk past where the car is parked.

To remove the dog's fear of getting into the car the best plan is to offer all meals inside it while it is stationary for two weeks. Simply lift your dog gently into the car and place its food bowl in with it. You can sit in the driver's seat for the first few days but do not start the engine. Allow your dog fifteen minutes to eat its food and then remove your dog together with any uneaten food. No food is offered until the next meal is due, when the process is repeated. If the dog eats very little on the first day then make sure that on the second day you put some extra-tasty food in your dog's bowl to encourage him to eat. Feeding from your hand while you reassure him is also helpful if your dog's fear overcomes its desire to eat. At the end of the first week you should be able to put your dog in the car with its food and leave it by itself for ten minutes to eat.

The next part of the sequence is to put the dog into the car holding the food bowl in your hand, start the engine and wait for a few seconds before offering the food. If your dog is reluctant to eat now that the engine is running and appears apprehensive, wait for five minutes and then switch off the engine and allow the dog a further ten minutes to eat. If you repeat this every day, when the dog will happily eat its food while the engine is running you can go through the motions of driving, i.e. use the indicators, gear change, rev up the engine, etc. without actually moving forward at all. You should now offer titbits only when your dog gets into the car, followed by more titbits when the dog comes out of the car, followed by an exercise session so that the dog getting into the car is always followed by exercise. Now that you have started the theme of making the act of getting into the car a pleasant experience and the prelude to exercise, it is a simple matter then to use the car every day for two weeks to take your dog for a short drive (the shorter the better) to the local park or exercise area.

Travel sickness

Quite a lot of young dogs suffer from travel motion sickness, although most owners overcome this by making frequent short trips to get the dog gradually used to this motion. The symptoms are general lethargy followed by drooling and vomiting.

If, after you have tried making lots of very short journeys, your dog is showing no signs of improvement then you can try all of the following techniques to reduce and, with luck, eliminate the problem.

1. Try to position your dog on the floor between the front and rear seats. This should help to reduce the motion of the car, particularly the rolling, side-to-side motion.
2. If you place a cushion on either side of your dog this will

also help to reduce the rocking motion that is so often the cause of travel sickness.

3. Try to plan exposure to car travel at times when the dog's stomach is reasonably empty.

4. In extreme cases it is often the actual smell of the car that is part of the association, so providing the bedding from the dog's basket for it to lie on can be beneficial in altering the background smell.

5. Finally, your vet will advise you on the use of medication in order to help your dog overcome the problem.

Over-excitement

Out of all of the problem behaviour associated with car travel the dog that jumps around barking and screaming with excitement is one of the most difficult for owners to cope with. As always, in order to overcome the problem it is important that you attempt to understand the cause.

The usual cause is the owner making the mistake of allowing the dog to associate car travel with free running exercise at the end of the journey. The dog is put into the car each day and driven to the local park where it is often allowed to jump out, race around and play. This then becomes the highlight of its life with the car journey being responsible for the build-up of excitement. When the owner gets to the stage where they now occasionally take the dog to the local shops, etc., where it does not get out of the car, the problem rapidly becomes worse. This is because the dog is now getting a reward of exercise and play that becomes unpredictable, and behaviour where a reward is produced at random is the most difficult to extinguish. This process is fully explained in my previous book, *Your Dog: Its Development, Behaviour and Training*.

To cure the behaviour takes more than a little effort and persistence on the owner's part, particularly if more than one dog is involved (see Chapter 6, Owning More than One Dog). The cure is applied in three stages.

Stage 1

You must continue to take your dog to the area that produces the maximum amount of excitement each day and try to ignore your dog's behaviour. Restricting the dog's movement by putting it into a travelling cage will certainly help. When you arrive at the area and stop the car, wait for five to ten minutes without allowing the dog to get out, then start the car and drive home without saying a word. When you arrive home be really cool and off-hand with your dog by reducing any attention it may receive.

You should also take it on as many other short journeys as possible but never letting the dog get out of the car until you arrive home. This must be carried out for one week, during which time the dog is allowed only lead exercise.

Stage 2

For the second week, you should walk your dog on a lead to the exercise area and allow it to play and run free. When you return home, put it in the car and drive it back to the exercise area. Do not allow your dog out of the car, wait ten minutes and then drive home.

Continue making short journeys as often as possible without allowing your dog to get out of the car. Continue for a further week.

Stage 3

Continue walking your dog to the exercise area on the lead (the exercise will do you good!), allowing it to run free if possible. Plan one or two journeys to this exercise area which now do not coincide with your lead exercise time. Before putting your dog into the car, spend twenty minutes playing with it in the garden or in the house. Try to pick a game or toy that produces the maximum amount of excitement. Then take your dog out to the exercise area without allowing it out of the car. By the end of this week you should have noticed a dramatic reduction in the dog's excitement in the car, because car journeys are now becoming boring affairs.

Stage 4

All free running exercise still takes place after walking to the area on the lead. Play which is designed to take the edge off the dog's enthusiasm and excitement *always* precedes car journeys. You can now occasionally get your dog out of the car for a short walk on the lead, which you can make less interesting for your dog by training it to lie down and stay while on the lead. It is generally accepted that control exercises reduce the dog's enthusiasm.

Stage 5

You can now occasionally allow free running exercise following a car journey, but try not always to use the same area otherwise the excitement will quickly start to build up again.

When your dog views the play that precedes the car journey as the highlight of its day and the exercise that follows the journey simply exercise and little else, then the problem should never manifest itself again.

Sadly for a lot of dogs, the owners play with their dogs so little in the house and garden that the park or field represents the highlight of the dog's whole life, making the ensuing excitement in the car leading up to exercise understandable from the dog's point of view.

Aggression problems in the car

These are dealt with in Chapter 7, Dog/Human Aggression Problems.

Jumping up/biting fingers, arms etc.

This is yet another case where prevention is better than cure and it is only because puppies are allowed and encouraged to jump up and sometimes not discouraged from biting their owners' fingers and arms that the problem starts to develop.

It is a very simple matter to retrain the dog not to jump up at its owners but it is much more difficult to stop the unwanted behaviour with visitors. This is because you are often dependent on your visitors using the same technique as you yourself apply in curing the problem.

Jumping up with the possible addition of finger/arm biting is at its worst in moments of extreme excitement such as someone in the family returning home or a well-known friend arriving in the house. The process of reversing the dog's behaviour relies on the owners starting off the required modification, which must be carried out consistently in order to be effective. It is unfair on the dog to allow it to jump up today because you are in a good mood but punish it for exactly the same behaviour tomorrow when you may be in a bad mood. So the rule has to be made clear to everyone in the family and to all visitors that the dog is not allowed to jump up ever again, whatever the reason.

We will first of all look at three corrective techniques to stop the behaviour and then look at substituting an acceptable behaviour in place of the unwanted one. All of the corrective methods rely on environmental correction rather than the correction appearing to come from the owner.

Method 1

Encourage your dog to jump up, particularly when it gets excited. When it does so hold on to its front paws and continue to do so but totally ignore it by looking away and not speaking to it. Do not let it get down again until it starts to become really uncomfortable and struggles to pull its paws free. You can then release your hold and allow it to get down. Immediately encourage it to jump up again and repeat the process as often as necessary until your dog declines your invitation to jump up. As soon as it reaches this decision and keeps all four feet on the floor for more than five seconds, really go to town and fuss and praise your dog. The chances are that this will now produce the unwanted behaviour of jumping up all over again, so you simply repeat the process of ignoring and holding when the dog jumps up and reward and give lots of attention to the dog when it is standing or, better still, sitting in front of you.

When you have reached the stage (usually within a week) where your dog greets you by standing or sitting in front of you for your praise instead of jumping up, you will need to show all your visitors how to continue the process that you have started. I can assure you that you will need to be far more persistent with your friends and relatives than you needed to be with your dog, but if they will not carry out your instructions you will end up with a dog that jumps up uncontrollably at anyone but your family.

Method 2
Used on dogs that are not concerned about remaining on their
hind legs for lengthy periods. Simply repeat Method 1 but now
extend one foot and *gently* place it over one of your dog's hind
paws, *slowly* increasing the pressure until it jumps down and
spins round to see what was causing the problem. Praise and
fuss when all four feet remain in contact with the ground, and
re-apply the correction and ignoring when the dog jumps back
up. Please note that only sufficient pressure must be progressively applied to make the dog get down. Under no circumstances must you stamp or tread down hard with your foot.

Method 3
This is used for dogs which not only jump up but tend to grip
hands and clothing with their teeth as well.

Invest in a water pistol and simply squirt the dog on the nose
when it jumps up; praise it when it has all four feet in contact
with the floor. You can also have an old glove or slipper at hand
to give the dog to hold on to when it starts to understand that it
is to remain standing or sitting in front of you when you fuss it.

This is particularly effective for gundogs who like to greet
their owners by carrying something in their mouths.

Visitors can be instructed to carry out the same procedure if
you leave a water pistol and glove near the front door.

Unfortunately, with some dogs water alone is not sufficient
to prevent the behaviour enough to allow positive reinforcement with the glove, slipper, toy, etc. for the correct behaviour.
In such a case you can try using a taste deterrent, taking care to
follow the manufacturer's instructions.

Fear

My definition of fear is an association or series of associations
linked with an extremely unpleasant experience. This unpleasant experience can be either real or imaginary and is
linked to a feeling of impending danger. So we can have a dog
that is frightened of going to the vet's because the first two visits
resulted in the disagreeable experience of inoculations, or we
can have a dog that is frightened of jet aircraft flying over even

though it has not had any unpleasant experiences with jet aircraft! The process of reducing fear or apprehension requires frequent exposure to all of the fear associations, initially at a very low level which is slowly and progressively increased.

The biggest problem is that quite often what the owner believes the dog is frightened of is not what the dog is actually frightened of at all. The best example that I can quote is a dog that was apparently gun-shy, that is frightened by the sound of a starting pistol going off. This happened for the first time in the competition exercise of steadiness to gunshot where the dog was required to walk at heel with its handler past the judge, who then fired two shots of a starting pistol in rapid succession. The dog was startled and spun round, glanced at the judge then ran away, and it took some time for the owner to regain control of the dog and calm it down.

The handler then, under my guidance, went through a two-week course of intensive training to overcome the problem. Basically this was achieved by getting someone to fire a starting pistol in the distance so that the dog received a very low-level 'dose' of noise. This was immediately followed by the handler throwing a toy, thus making the almost indiscernible noise the prelude to an exceptionally exciting event for the dog – playing with a toy that the dog was crazy about. We gradually got the gun nearer and nearer over a period of fourteen days until the dog would quite happily walk to heel with its handler past me while I repeatedly fired the gun, whereupon the handler would throw the toy.

At the next competition, not only did the dog run off again when the gun was fired but he was also showing signs of fear during other exercises that did not appear to have any associations with the gun.

We repeated the de-sensitising process and although the dog was unconcerned when the gun was fired in training at the next competition, he refused to do heelwork near the judge even though the gun had not been fired. We even went to the extent of trying to get the dog to play with the gun in training, which presented no problems. I was stumped and suggested that the fear was being transmitted by the owner (which is often given as a cause when we don't know the answer). Then quite by chance I happened to be standing on the training field with a clipboard in my hand and to our mutual surprise the dog would not come anywhere near me. It was the clipboard and not the gun that the dog was frightened of!

What I surmised with hindsight had happened was that when the dog had received its first fright in competition and turned round in the direction of the noise, what it had seen was a white sheet of paper on a clipboard. The dog had naturally assumed that the noise had come from there. It is only we with our thinking minds who would know that the noise could have come only from the gun. In trying to correct the problem we had de-sensitised the dog to the sound of the gun but had completely missed the fact that we also needed to de-sensitise it to the sight of the clipboard!

Repeating the toy-throwing past and over the clipboard on the ground, placing toys on a clipboard, and having a person stand with a clipboard and throw a toy from on top of it as the dog approached without ever firing a gun in training totally eliminated the problem and it has never recurred under either competition or training conditions.

Systematic de-sensitisation

This is the fancy name that we use to describe the process of gradually overcoming fear-associated problems by applying the following techniques.

Stage 1

First of all try to establish precisely what the dog is frightened of, remembering that your view may not coincide with the dog's view. You may need to do this by a process of elimination. To help you do this, ask yourself the following questions.

a) Is the dog's fear linked with a series of events such as heelwork + gunfire + clipboard = fear, as in the previous example? If it is, then quite often the first part of the series of associations may produce a fear reaction, i.e. simply doing heelwork may prove stressful if the dog is expecting it to progress to the fearful experience of the gun being fired.

b) Is the dog's fear linked in any way with a particular area? In other words, if the dog was subjected to the sound of the gun while walking through an area of woodland then it may be apprehensive about any future excursion into any woods or specifically frightened only to enter the particular woods where the gun was fired.

c)   What was your reaction to the dog's fear? Is it possible that by fussing and coaxing your dog you are compounding the dog's fear by your own positive reinforcement (reward) for the fear that the dog has shown? Were you frightened by the experience? If so, the dog should be happier if the sequence leading up to the fright is repeated but this time with someone else accompanying the dog.

Stage 2

Subject the dog to frequent exposures to whatever you believe it to be frightened of at an extremely low level. So if it is frightened of thunderstorms you can make a start by purchasing the BBC Sound Effects Record Number 1, which has a very realistic thunderstorm on it along with gunfire, jet aircraft, helicopter, trains, etc. Play this on a good stereo system as often as possible each day. You can record the track you need on both sides of a tape over and over again and then play it back at the lowest level possible while feeding your dog or playing with it with a toy.

When the dog starts to accept the fact that the tape is playing and ceases to take notice of it, you can play it more frequently so that it becomes 'background noise' and part of a normal daily occurrence. If you then slowly and progressively start to increase the volume on a daily or, in extreme cases, a weekly basis you should eventually de-sensitise the dog to the sound within the area where you have carried out the conditioning. Always reward the behaviour you want and try to ignore any unwanted behaviour.

Stage 3

The next stage is to change the association of the environment in which you have carried out the conditioning. So you will need to repeat the process in as many areas as you possibly can otherwise your dog may well learn to accept the sound of thunderstorms in your own house but may wreck the car trying to escape the next time you leave him in the car when it hears thunder in the distance.

Stage 4

Progressively reduce the frequency of the reward you give your dog each time you subject it to the stimulus, but increase the content of the reward. This ensures that if the dog is subjected to the fearful experience and you are not on hand to reward it for correct behaviour, it will not interfere with the dog's progress. Random rewards once a behaviour has been learnt are by far the most effective.

Specific sound can, of course, be recorded at source on a portable cassette recorder where commercially produced sound-tracks are not available.

You should bear in mind that your own attitude is extremely important and if you continue as if nothing has happened when your dog exhibits any signs of fear without advertising the fact that your dog's fear has got you worried in any way, then your dog should gain strength and courage from you.

Fear is made worse for the dog when the event happens at random and becomes unpredictable. Thus the dog never has the chance to come to terms with its fear. You can liken this to someone who has a fear of spiders. If a spider walked across your living-room floor at precisely seven o'clock every evening and followed the same path, even if you were terrified at first, after several days you would be able to predict when it would occur and either take avoiding action in the form of not sitting in its path or even dismiss it as being of no concern to you as it has never tried to approach you personally. If something really pleasant happened each evening which coincided with the appearance of the spider you might actually start to look forward to seeing it. The reason people are frightened of spiders is that in addition to their appearance, they turn up in the most unpredictable places at random. You only need once to reach out to take a book off the bookshelf and find a spider perched on top of it and you would be ultra careful each time you subsequently took a book off that shelf. This is because the presence of the fright was totally unpredictable. In order for the technique of de-sensitisation to work the event has to appear to be predictable and linked with something pleasant.

Sadly for the dog, the process of de-sensitisation is more usually carried out to teach the dog to accept punishment on a regular basis than it is used to cure behaviour problems.

Finally, if you have a dog that is really terrified of thunderstorms where it is not only the sound but also the atmospheric changes that affect the dog, then by providing it with a safe refuge such as a dark cupboard under the stairs or another dark enclosed area you will go some way towards reducing the dog's fear.

Sedatives administered by your vet will also help in extreme cases of fear-related problems.

10

You, the Owner

Although this book has been written to enable owners to be in a better position to understand the requirements of their dogs in order either to socialise them, to train them or to modify any unacceptable aspects of their behaviour, we have really examined only one half of the partnership in any great detail. I would estimate around eight out of ten owners will have some kind of behaviour problems with their pet dog, with most of these being very minor in nature. I would also estimate that this figure is far greater for dogs that have behaviour problems with their owners, although fortunately again most are minor in nature.

The majority of problems are the result of a breakdown in communications between man and dog, and now that we are moving into a new age of technology and improving our own ability to communicate with one another with the written word, speech and even visual body language over vast distances on a global scale we are slowly losing our instinctive ability to communicate with our number-one companion animal.

I firmly believe that there are some people among us who have a feeling for dogs and can appear immediately to strike up an understanding and a working relationship with even the most difficult of dogs. Their skill is not learnt from attending seminars, reading books or studying at college or university but is learnt from living with dogs.

We all tend to look for easy answers or miracle cures and want other people to solve our problems for us when the answers are there within all of us if only we can learn to look deeply enough at ourselves and at our dogs.

We are now living for the most part within a society geared towards the consumer, with our dogs becoming an increasingly consumable commodity. Dogs are often purchased without even a fraction of the thought that would go into buying a new car. The dog, however, is required to live up to much higher expectations than any car would ever have to and with less input and maintainance from the owner.

Before you can go out and drive a car alone on the public highway you have to be taught the skills necessary and you are also required to take a test. Not so with a dog. You can own a dog for a lifetime without ever having to understand what makes it work. When problems occur with your car you can pay to have it fixed or if it fails to come up to expectations you can simply trade it in for another model. If you start to have problems with your dog's behaviour, again you can pay someone to 'fix' them, hence the sudden explosion of training kennels and behaviour consultants, or you can pass the dog on to a welfare organisation or rescue centre and go out and get another one that you hope will fulfil your requirements.

There is also the breaker's yard for your car when the problems become too expensive to fix and the car is old. Sadly, there are more young, fit dogs euthanased (put to sleep) than old dogs because problems have been allowed to develop which the owner sees as insurmountable. Young dogs have been euthanased for no better reason than that they have shed hairs on the furniture.

For the most part we are unwilling to devote the time and effort necessary to educate our dogs but are intolerant of the resulting bad behaviour we experience, although we expect the dogs to tolerate our own bad behaviour and to conform to our own standards.

Worse than that, we are now in the habit of selecting pet dogs to fit into a family environment that are of a much higher specification than our actual requirements.

The trend is towards bigger dogs with some working ability bred into them, and also dual dog ownership seems to be on the increase. Does an average pet-dog owner really want or need a dog in the living room that was bred to hunt lions and that *still retains this ability*? Should the owning of certain breeds be restricted to exhibiters and enthusiasts only? I feel that through our own ignorance we will soon witness the decline of the family pet and see the right to own dogs of certain breeds restricted even more. Incidentally, I should perhaps mention that my wife and I were made homeless on two occasions many years ago by refusing to give up the right to own our dogs.

So how can we ensure that a companion dog does not turn into a problem dog and a liability which will add fuel to the growing anti-dog campaign?

First of all, you should do your homework and make sure that you and the family are going to live up to your dog's expectations of you. Without devoting time to education and training you will almost certainly be heading for trouble, for make no mistake about it, your dog is quite able to educate itself if you fail to take the initiative. Lots of pet dogs actually do a much better job of training their owners than you would ever think possible.

Take, for instance, a dog that has trained its owner to offer ever more tasty morsels of food simply by going over to its bowl, sniffing and then turning up its nose and walking away. Or how about the dog that has trained its owner never to go out of the house and leave it? I often see dogs in the local park that have trained their owners to fetch sticks or to play games of chase!

Some owners, it must be said, are quite happy to fit into their dog's pack, accepting that the dog is number one and allowing it all the privileges afforded to its rank. They feed the dog when it tells them to, are happy to allow it to sleep anywhere it chooses, touch it when told, leave it alone when it tells them to. If the owner does anything to upset the dog and it growls at them they immediately apologise and show signs of submission by offering gifts. The dog is never a real problem for its owners because they have learnt all the signs, signals and body language so ably taught them by their dog and so know how to avoid situations that result in confrontation.

I see a great number of owners who tell me their dog's behaviour is unpredictable, but believe me I see a far greater number of dogs who tell me that their owner's behaviour is unpredictable. Most dogs tell me that 95 per cent of the time their owners are loving and affectionate but the other 5 per cent of the time they become aggressive, their eyes glaze over and they start to growl and show their teeth for no apparent reason! This is because the owner assumes that when the dog is punished for some minor crime it will associate the punishment with whatever preceded it – a few might but most will not if the time difference between crime and punishment is more than about four seconds. They will simply associate their owner's sudden change of behaviour with the action of punishment. That is why owners frequently tell me that their dogs know when they are in a bad mood!

Take a typical example of food stealing. The dog steals food and the owner notices this while the dog is in the act of eating its bounty, rushes towards the dog screaming and shouting abuse and then smacks it half a dozen times. Put yourself in the position the dog is now in. Is it not possible that you will learn that stealing food when your owner is in the same room produces a sudden, inexplicably aggressive reaction in him or her? If that is the case you will simply learn to avoid stealing food when your owner is in view and you will progress to stealing food when your owner is not around to be aggressive. This is, in fact, what the majority of dogs learn. They do not dare go near food when the owner is present because they are frightened of the owner becoming aggressive. When the owner goes out for a few minutes everything in sight is eaten!

Some dogs will link their owner's aggression with the competition over who gets to eat the spoils, with the result that the dog still steals food in view of its owners but learns to bolt down the food much more quickly before the owner gets too close.

Other dogs will believe that they are being punished for allowing themselves to be caught and will continue stealing but get better at avoiding their aggressive owners! The chance of the dog learning that it must never steal food again, even if the owner is not present and whatever the circumstances, is at best remote. Even if the dog did in fact learn never to steal food again, the process of learning would be based on fear of the owner, which is not exactly the best way of maintaining a close relationship.

This is where the concept of environmental punishment comes in.

Environmental correction

This is where the dog receives correction from the environment, or more specifically from the activity that we want to extinguish. Using food stealing as an example, the trick is to make the correction come from the dog's act of stealing and from the food rather than from the owner. This is simply done by placing a metal tea-tray upright behind the plate of food and having a bunch of keys at hand ready to throw. When the dog walks over to steal the food, throw the keys to strike the tray just at the moment he goes to open his mouth to steal the food. The dog must not hear you warn him or be facing you when the keys are thrown. We want the act of stealing the food itself to be mildly unpleasant. Applied correctly you will dissuade the dog from stealing the food but not link the unpleasantness with the owner. In fact, you can appear to be most sympathetic to your dog once it receives the little shock. If you then repeat the process once or twice more you will very quickly teach the dog that it is never safe to touch the food whether you are there or not, and more to the point you will remain your dog's best friend and not its worst enemy.

Far too many dogs go through life constantly looking over their shoulder to see what sort of mood their owners are in from hour to hour and day to day.

Systematic de-sensitisation to correction

The process of systematic de-sensitisation discussed in the previous chapter with regard to correcting fear-associated problems is more often used by pet-dog owners to de-sensitise their dogs to both physical and verbal punishment. Even in formal training classes owners are taught how to de-sensitise their dogs to the effects of collars, followed by check chains.

It works like this: wait until the dog does something of which you disapprove and then corner it and give it a mild ticking-off. Start off by doing this at a very low, quiet level, lasting for just a few seconds. Then, each time the dog repeats its undesirable behaviour, repeat the process but slowly and systematically increase the volume and duration of the threats you shout at your dog. You will in a very short space of time have taught your dog to accept and ignore any sort of verbal abuse that you are able to direct towards it. You have systematically de-sensitised it to shouting and threatening and it would be extremely unlikely that you could stop it from engaging in anything of which you disapprove by telling it off.

Physical punishment works the same way. Start off by putting the dog in the position where it cannot escape and begin by tapping the dog gently on the nose with one finger on the first few occasions it does anything wrong. Then steadily and progressively increase the severity of the punishment and you will end up with a dog that will still misbehave even if you give it a severe beating, which you have taught it to accept as the normal daily pattern of life. This is why people need to resort to spiked chains and electric collars because they have run out of other severe forms of punishment and cannot hurt the dog enough using smacks or jerks on a chain as a means of obtaining a behaviour modification.

So whenever physical or verbal punishment is considered it should always be as a last resort and must be carried out at a sufficiently high level to produce the desired effect, on the basis that it will be used only on exceptionally rare occasions.

It's strange to observe that oppressive techniques of punishing undesirable behaviour, rather than the creative system of ignoring undesirable behaviour and rewarding good behaviour, tend to be in widespread use in bringing up both children and dogs.

Owner motivation

In order to bring up and subsequently train a dog correctly it is important that there is no lack of motivation on the owner's part. This becomes even more important when the question of altering any of their dog's undesirable behaviour arises. Dogs rarely change without some external influence from their owners and so to effect a change in behaviour the owner must want to make it happen. How successful any behaviour-modification programme is will be directly dependent on how committed the owners are in wanting to change things. It is for this reason more than any other that I try to structure my programmes of behaviour modification into stages, usually set at weekly or fortnightly intervals.

So when dog owners realise and accept that their dog's behaviour is giving cause for concern and take steps to obtain help in sorting out their problems, part of the battle is already over. I plan the first stage of any programme to ensure that the owner is in a position to achieve some small credit for improving things, and it is to be hoped that they will then be encouraged to continue with the later and sometimes more difficult stages. The owners are thus positively reinforced for their achievements.

Sometimes, if you try to make too many changes too quickly in either the dog's environment or the rules under which it is to continue life within the family, you get a temporary worsening of its behaviour. This is occasionally enough to tip the owners over the edge and they immediately give up. So the first rule is to set realistic goals that can be easily achieved in the early stages. Progress throughout the programme should be positively reinforced by everyone involved with assisting the owner, whether it be the behaviour consultant, vet, breeder or trainer. The more support that is offered, the better the owner is able to cope and continue to work through the entire programme.

I am always prepared to modify my basic programmes at any stage to take into account the individual nature of each dog and owner I am working with if the programme appears to be ineffective or is proving difficult to apply. Sometimes by trying to see a problem from the dog's viewpoint will give you a totally different outlook and approach.

Take, for instance, a problem I was presented with relating to a dog that became obsessed about picking up sticks in the local park and running around with them in its mouth. At first the owner did not see this as much of a problem – indeed, it meant that at first the dog would amuse itself without requiring any input from the owner at all. The problem became apparent when the dog had to receive veterinary treatment to a damaged mouth on two occasions when it had injured itself by racing around and bumping into things with a stick between its teeth, to say nothing of the obvious dangers of a stick being pushed into its throat and perforating its windpipe. The owner wrote that although the dog was mildly interested in playing with one or two toys that were available in the house, it refused to play with its toys when taken out for a walk, preferring its preoccupation with sticks.

As this was an interesting exercise I gave the problem to a class of pupils whom I was instructing on a dog-behaviour course. Most of them came up with variations on the same basic cure, which was the following.

a) Exercise the dog in stick-free areas for a couple of weeks.
b) Remove the dog's constant right of access to the toys at home and teach the dog to play with them for short spells before putting them away again.
c) Stop the dog playing all games with toys in the house and take it out to your stick-free area and encourage it to play with its toys.
d) Prepare a few sticks with a coating of taste deterrent and place in the exercise area. Take out a favourite toy and encourage the dog to play with it. If it tries to pick up a stick it will get an unpleasant taste in its mouth, hopefully unpleasant enough to stop the behaviour.

My own approach to the problem was based on making a few observations and asking a few questions, as follows.

a) *Question:* Why does the dog not want to play with its toys outside the house?
    Answer: It can play with toys whenever it wants to, twenty-four hours each day, and so the excitement induced by the production of one of these toys would be negligible.
b) *Question:* Why does the dog enjoy playing with sticks so much?
    Answer: Because it can have access to these more exciting toys only twice each day for a short period on each occasion.
c) *Question:* How can you make the dog more interested in the toys outside the house?
    Answer: By withholding them inside the house so that they are used only outside, where they quickly become as exciting as the sticks.
d) *Question:* How can you make the sticks less interesting when outside?

Answer: Bring the sticks into the house and leave them lying around for the dog to play with twenty-four hours a day so that the excitement that they produce becomes negligible!

The majority of behaviour problems that exist in our dogs really are that simple to deal with providing you are prepared to sit and think about them and ask your dog a few simple questions.

Everything I do in my work with dogs is relatively simple and straightforward and follows a very logical path. The response I get from most owners of 'problem' dogs is, 'It's all so logical now that you have explained it to me.' So you see that there are no miracle cures, just plain common sense based on an enormous amount of personal observations of dogs and owners in their natural habitat.

Try to remember that although we speak a different language from our dogs and they may pose a lot of questions in terms of their behaviour, they also hold all the answers if we only take the trouble to talk to them on a level which they can understand.

Throughout this book I have attempted to explain all the reasons behind your dog's behaviour, and as you will appreciate, this has had to be confined to very general terms. Dogs, however, are as individual as their owners and it is for this reason that before you attempt to put any of my suggestions into practice, you must be absolutely certain that you know what problem your dog actually has. It would be unwise to base an attempted behaviour modification on mere guesswork, as any such attempt would almost certainly be doomed to failure.

Although I have tried to base all my work on rewarding good behaviour rather than punishing bad behaviour, I have had to include techniques that could arguably lead to placing the dog under minor, controlled amounts of stress. This is only ever done if other techniques have failed, or experience has shown that they would be likely to be ineffective. Everything has to be seen in perspective and any method using corrective techniques can obviously be open to abuse if it is applied either incorrectly or carried out to excess.

Throughout your dog's lifetime it is always much easier to

prevent problems from arising rather than to correct the problem after you have allowed it to become established in the first place. The longer a problem is left and the more it has been allowed to develop, the harder it will be to correct, and for this reason it is important that advice is sought at the first signs that something is amiss.

Vets, behaviour therapists and trainers

Throughout this book I have stressed the importance of a thorough preliminary examination by a qualified vet in order to eliminate behaviour problems having any obvious (or not so obvious) physical cause. There are more vets now showing an interest in assisting owners with behaviour therapy and it may be that you are lucky enough to be the client of such a practice. If not, your vet will, if he or she feels it necessary, refer you to a behaviour therapist in your area who will be a member of the Association of Pet Behaviour Consultants.

This Association of like-minded individuals, all with a professional interest in pet behaviour problems, was founded in 1989 to promote a common code of practice when assisting clients who are experiencing problems with their pets.

Founder members, John Fisher, Peter Neville, David Appleby and myself, have now been joined by Dr Valerie O'Farrell and Dr Ian Dunbar as well as several other eminent animal behaviourists.

The letters A.P.B.C are your guarantee of professional competence. You can obtain further information from the Secretary, Association of Pet Behaviour Consultants, 50 Pall Mall London SW 1.

An initial consultation with a dog-behaviour therapist will usually take place in the form of a telephone call. Sometimes it is possible to offer advice over the phone for some minor problems, although usually if the problem involves aggression an appointment will need to be made to take your dog along to a 'clinic' for a detailed consultation and behaviour-modification programme tailored to your individual dog. In the vast majority of cases a single visit lasting approximately one to two hours will be all that is necessary, although complex or long-standing problems may require further visits.

If you have no problems with your dog's overall behaviour but would simply like to learn to improve your control over your dog or teach it a few useful training exercises, then your local library will be able to give you details of any training classes near to where you live.

It is not a particularly good idea to take along a dog that has aggression problems to a session with other people and their dogs as in the enclosed environment of a training class you may find that your dog's behaviour starts to deteriorate or that he begins to create aggression problems for other dog owners. Control training with an aggressive dog should always be an addition to behaviour therapy and not a substitute for it. But there is absolutely no reason why even the most aggressive of dogs cannot join in the fun of a training class once the problems of aggression have been sorted out.

Finally, during the years that I have spent working with and observing dogs I have been indebted to all the dogs and people who have allowed me the benefit of their knowledge and experience. I, for my part, have no secrets that I am not willing to share with anyone who may express an interest.

With the increasing amount of pressure being placed on the domestic dog from all corners of life, the need for a better understanding of the art of both verbal and non-verbal communication between man and dog has never been greater. The only 'experts' on dogs are the dogs themselves.

Index